Presented to Abhiroop lal

with best wishe

Jan 10th 2019.

"Rami Ranger has consistently distinguished himself as one of the UK's leading entrepreneurs. Throughout his long career he has singled himself out as a leading businessman and a campaigner for social reform, with the numerous accolades for his company, Sun Mark, being just one example of his entrepreneurial zeal."

Lord Bilimoria of Chelsea
Founder and chairman of Cobra Beer

"I cannot believe that anyone before has risen from so low to the heights now occupied by Rami Ranger. There may never have been a more inspirational book than this – a 'must read' by one of the greatest of modern entrepreneurs."

Stephen Pound MP
Member of Parliament for Ealing North

"[He has] demonstrated true leadership, sharing his enthusiasm with his staff, rewarding success and driving growth through a strong customer-centric approach [and] an inspirational ethical outlook on his business."

Institute of Directors
On awarding Rami Ranger the 2013 award for Director of the Year – Large Company

"Rami is a tremendous businessman, an inspiring philanthropist and a kind-hearted gentleman. What he lacked in terms of a formal education, he has more than made up for with effort, determination and entrepreneurial skill. He has helped to make Britain a better and more successful place and I am delighted he has taken the time to tell his story."

Lord Popat of Harrow

"Rami's story is unique – a martyred father – a childhood of struggle – a flair for enterprise and innovation and a deep, deep sense of community and service. But his character is even more exceptional than his story."

Barry Gardiner MP
Shadow Minister for the Natural Environment & Fisheries
Member of Parliament for Brent North

"Rami Ranger has led an extraordinary life. He has overcome tragedy and adversity to become one of the UK's best known and most successful businessmen."

Baroness Jenkin of Kennington

"Rami Ranger's success comes from within himself. His approach to life is one of hard work, imagination, self-confidence, and strong friendships. His achievements have been breath-taking."

James Arbuthnot MP
Chairman of the Defence Select Committee
Member of Parliament for North East Hampshire

"From humble beginnings he has reached great heights ... He is a fine example for all of us in the community and a great credit to this country."

Lord Paul of Marylebone

"A true servant of Britain in so many capacities – I can only imagine he never sleeps."

Chloe Smith MP
Member of Parliament for Norwich North

"One of our country's greatest business minds and leaders. His business vision and global success is immense and he is the embodiment of so many values that we British Asians all hold dear."

Priti Patel MP
Member of Parliament for Witham

"Rami came to Britain with practically nothing and yet has managed to build up one of the most successful exporting companies in the country."

Sir Tony Baldry MP
Second Church Estates Commissioner
Member of Parliament for Banbury

"Rami, through his story, is a role model for many people living around the world – his life shows that it doesn't matter what your background is; with the right commitment anyone has the chance to succeed if they follow their ambitions."

Paul Uppal MP
Member of Parliament for Wolverhampton South West

"His life has been extraordinary and he is an inspiration for others to follow."

Lord Sheikh of Cornhill

FROM NOTHING TO EVERYTHING

eBook edition

As a buyer of the print edition of *From Nothing to Everything* you can download the eBook edition free of charge to read on an eReader, smartphone, tablet or computer. Simply go to:

ebooks.harriman-house.com/ fromnothingtoeverything

Or point your smartphone at the QRC code here.

You can then register and download your free eBook.

FROM NOTHING TO EVERYTHING

An inspiring saga of struggle and success
from £2 to a £200 million business

DR RAMI RANGER MBE, FRSA

HARRIMAN HOUSE LTD

3A Penns Road

Petersfield

Hampshire

GU32 2EW

GREAT BRITAIN

Tel: +44 (0)1730 233870

Email: enquiries@harriman-house.com

Website: www.harriman-house.com

First published in Great Britain in 2014.

Copyright © Harriman House Ltd.

The right of Rami Ranger to be identified as the Author has been asserted in accordance with the Copyright, Designs and Patents Act 1988.

Co-authored by Simon Wicks.

ISBN: 9780857192585

British Library Cataloguing in Publication Data

A CIP catalogue record for this book can be obtained from the British Library.

FOREWORD
BY JOHN BERCOW

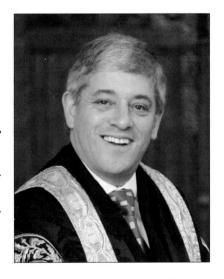

ALBERT EINSTEIN ONCE said "strive not to be a success, but rather to be of value". Dr Rami Ranger MBE, however, aspired to be both. And as this book illustrates, his endeavour has been a success.

Rami Ranger's story is one of triumph in the face of adversity. Having arrived in London after his family fled India in 1971 in the face of increasing tension, Rami has well and truly made his mark in the UK.

This book chronicles Rami's achievements and the mountains he has had to climb to reach his self-set goals. His story is inspiring and motivational, and one which tells of a man's tireless determination to thrive.

As chairman of two of the fastest-growing export businesses in the country, Rami's contribution to the British economy has rightly been honoured with numerous Queen's Awards. Having established himself as a respected business leader, Rami has put his heritage and experience to good use, working across a number of organisations to raise the profile of Asians in Britain, as well as leading a campaign to highlight the contribution of the Hindu community to British society. That leadership, and other achievements, saw him recognised with an MBE in 2005.

Rami's journey has seen him grow from living in a refugee camp to becoming a beacon of British society. Businessman, campaigner, philanthropist, Rami's story is remarkable. He deserves both our respect and our appreciation for what he has contributed to our country.

Rt Hon John Bercow MP

Speaker of the House of Commons
Member of Parliament for Buckingham

PREFACE

WHEN RAMI RANGER arrived in London in 1971 as a fresh-faced 23-year-old, he expected to find "streets that were paved with gold" in a nation where all-comers were welcomed with open arms. His fantasy of an easy life had been fuelled by the British cinema he watched as a child in India in the 1950s and 60s. The Britain depicted in the movies was a charming place where ordinary people spoke like the Queen and drove stylish two-seater sports cars. It was a land where the sun shone brightly, nothing too bad ever happened and everything was all right in the end.

What Rami imagined could hardly have been further from the truth. In fact, the naïve young immigrant found himself dropped into a society struggling to adjust to the postwar decline of its imperial status. Its economy was creaking under the weight of high inflation and industrial unrest. Work was hard to come by, particularly for a foreigner in a country where racial prejudice was casual and commonplace.

Shocked by the size of the chasm between what he imagined and what he found, the young Rami Ranger resolved to return home as soon as he could afford to.

That he didn't leave is testament to the strength of character instilled in him by a childhood spent battling hardship in post-independence India. Born into a Sikh family in what is now Pakistan just two months before the creation of the new Muslim state, Rami's earliest months were spent in turmoil. His father had been assassinated before his birth while trying to halt an attack on students campaigning against the division of India. His freshly-widowed mother fled amid chaos, with eight children in tow, to the relative safety of a refugee camp south of the new border.

They were among millions of Indians who left what was to become a Muslim state by whatever means they could. In the case of Rami's family, this meant sitting on the coal tender of a train for a full two days as the train crawled with agonising slowness through chaos, upheaval and desperation.

> "We were all black with the soot from the coal. My mother was black, my brothers and sister were black. I was black – although my brother tells me that I would turn blue with fright when the engine whistled loudly beside us and so pushed hankies in my ears to dampen the sound. Once we had arrived at Ferozepur station, we were so bedraggled with soot and dust that we were only just recognisable to my mother's brother, Faujdar Singh, who had come to collect us …

> " … I was born into the biggest migration of people in modern history. I was born into a world of division, disharmony and desperation. We had nothing then, not even a home."

Sixty-six years later and the baby on the coal tender has become the architect of one of Britain's fastest-growing and most decorated businesses, Sun Mark, and a leading figure in the UK's Asian community. Aside from building an international business that has won an unprecedented five successive Queen's Awards, Rami has worked tirelessly to foster better relations between the UK's Indian and Pakistani communities and to improve the profile of Asians in modern Britain. He has become a man who has the ear of senior members of government and the respect of British Asians whatever their religion, status or country of origin.

From Nothing to Everything tells the tale of this extraordinary journey from a refugee camp in post-independence India to the height of commercial and social success in modern Britain. Rami's words relate the life and thoughts of an inspirational man who has refused to give in, whatever the obstacles that confronted him – whether prejudice, betrayal of trust or depression brought on by the fatigue of fighting battles on all fronts.

During the course of telling his story, Rami describes the birth and growth of a business that has expanded at an astonishing rate throughout a global downturn in trade. He offers lessons in business and lessons in life that draw heavily on the values instilled in him as a child by a mother determined to create the best foundation for her children in the most trying of circumstances.

He reflects, too, on the ethics of good business, the importance of self-respect and his unquenchable ambition to build a worthwhile life for himself, his family and his community in a country he now considers home.

> "It's the logic of life: a man wants a suit and once he gets a suit, he wants another. When he feels he has enough suits, he wants a car; then he wants a bigger car, then a house, then a bigger house – and so on. His ambition grows with each new accomplishment. So my vision has expanded step by step."

From Nothing to Everything is not the tale of a rapid rise to recognition and reward, but rather a deeply personal account of the slow and certain trajectory towards a better life built on strong principles and solid foundations. In this sense, it is also the story of many Asian immigrants to the UK who have had to work hard and battle discrimination in order to become valued, accepted and, in some cases, influential members of British society.

What emerges above all from this self-portrait is an irrepressibly driven man who doesn't want merely to have everything but to be everything he can possibly be and who wants to make his mark on the world.

> "Nothing is ideal in this world but we have to make the most of what we have when we have it. In doing so, we should strive for whatever right we can do. If we do nothing, we achieve nothing."

As Rami himself might say, "Effort is in the hands of man, rewards are in the hand of God". Enjoy his story.

Harriman House

CONTENTS

PART I.
NOTHING

From Patiala to Thornton Heath

1. THE PROUDEST INDIAN MOTHER

WAS BORN on 3 July 1947 into a Sikh family in Gujranwala, now part of Pakistan, during the partition of India into two states after the second world war. My father, a prominent lawyer who campaigned against the break-up of our nation into states divided along religious lines, had been killed by pro-partition fanatics on 5 March. My mother was left alone with eight children aged from 2 to 14, including myself; a new-born, posthumous child.

We lived in Multan, a town that was to become part of Muslim Pakistan on 14 August 1947. Tension was high and violence had become commonplace. Like countless other non-Muslim families, we had to get out.

I have been told that the train we escaped on in the week before partition was so full that it was impossible for us to get on. The carriages were overflowing with people; there were many on the rooftop or hanging out of windows and off the sides. It was a desperate scene as the train prepared for its journey south to Ferozepur (which would remain part of India).

My mother with a baby in her arms and seven children trailing behind her grabbed a handle on the side of the engine and screamed at the driver. "You must help us!" she cried. "I am the wife of Shaheed Nanak Singh, who was assassinated for opposing the division of India. You must help us. Please!"

The engine driver recalled reading about the killing of Shaheed Nanak Singh in the newspaper and, such was my father's name, he took pity on us. "Look, I can't help you get on the train but if you don't mind you are welcome to sit on the coal tender," he said. "You know where that is?" So my mother sat with her children on the coals and our journey began.

We were all black with the soot from the coal. My mother was black, my brothers and sister were black. I was black – although my brother tells me that I would turn blue with fright when the engine whistled loudly beside us and so pushed hankies in my ears to dampen the sound. Once we had arrived at Ferozepur station, we were so bedraggled with soot and dust that we were only just recognisable to my mother's brother, Faujdar Singh, who had come to collect us.

My mother cried with relief when she saw him. The journey from Gujranwala to Ferozepur, normally a few hours, had taken three days. It had been anarchy: the train was constantly stopped and looted. Non-Muslims were, after all, refugees at the time and were easy targets for bandits on the road.

Men were beaten and women were raped. People were taken and not seen again. It was turmoil. The stories I've heard are horrific. But we survived. We stayed with my uncle in Ferozepur for a few days until floods forced yet another evacuation and we headed to Patiala. My mother had a sister there and the Maharajah had opened refugee camps for as many displaced people as could be crammed into them.

Our journey to Patiala is a story in its own right. My newly widowed mother took her eight children the 115 miles by bus, foot and *tanga* – a horse-drawn cart. By whatever means we could travel, we eventually arrived at a camp in Patiala, where we were finally able to rest. It was not long before we had to think about our next move.

This is how my life began. I was born into the biggest migration of people in modern history. I was born into a world of division, disharmony and desperation. We had nothing then, not even a home. My mother's horrific descriptions of these early days have never left my mind.

*   *   *   *

As the youngest of eight, I was a spoilt child. I was loved and cared for by everyone, especially by my mother, who thought of me as a gift after the killing of her husband and the loss of everything she knew. At the age of just 35, she had lost her husband, her ancestral home and her country. In addition, she had no means of making a living with eight children to feed, clothe and care for.

However, my mother was very resourceful and she wasn't going to give in, no matter what the fates had thrown at her. She was determined, courageous and she could improvise.

Whilst everybody else was trying to collect jewellery and other valuables during the evacuation from Multan, my mother was rescuing my father's papers – his certificates, writings, newspaper cuttings and any other documents where he had been mentioned. My father was highly respected and my mother knew the value in preserving his papers.

After a while in the refugee camp, she went to see the chief minister of Patiala and showed him the documents. "This is what I was and this is what I have become," she told him. "I need your help."

At that time there was also migration from India into the new state of Pakistan. Many Muslims had fled Patiala, leaving their houses empty. For a while, everyone thought this abandonment would be temporary and the owners would return. However, it soon became clear that this would not happen. The chief minister, empathising with my mother, sent two security guards with her into the town to find an empty house for our family. Once a suitable home was found, the men unlocked it and we took possession.

That was not all. The chief minister also asked my mother if she was educated. She explained that she had set up a primary school in rural Multan and taught village children alongside *memsahibs* (the British ladies who were part of the establishment in the British Raj). Impressed, the chief minister arranged a job for her in a nearby primary school where she could teach children aged five to eight. On top of that, he promised to give her own children free education. Once again, my father's reputation had earned us favours and, unlike many others, we were able to settle into a new home after spending just a few months in the refugee camp.

Our house was in a poorer part of the city, but it was a good one for us. It was brick-built and had three rooms over three storeys. We didn't have much furniture and at night the house became a dormitory with the nine of us sleeping where we could. We slept in cots made of bamboo, on *duri* (cotton mats), with just a cotton sheet in the summer and an extra blanket in winter.

Money was scarce when I was young and we were always struggling. Sometimes there was not enough for winter clothes or for the upkeep of the house, even though, as we got older, my brothers left home to join the Indian Army as commissioned officers and sent us money to help us financially.

For much of my childhood, we lived hand to mouth. A lot of people in our neighbourhood were refugees too. We were able to empathise with each other and survived partly through our own resourcefulness and partly through the kindness of others. For example, there was a particular shopkeeper who would extend my mother credit when she couldn't afford to pay for our food, because he knew that she was trustworthy. Looking back, I realise that we were extremely poor but, as it was all we knew, we accepted it as the norm at the time.

I never needed to be clever to survive because everything was put on a plate for me by my mother and siblings. I have never seen anyone work as hard as my mother did. When I look back at my childhood, I see my mother working from morning until evening. She used to wake up at four in the morning to cook breakfast for the family. She would leave the food for us to eat and then go to school to teach for the day. Then she'd come back from school and the process would start again – cooking dinner for the children, not to mention maintaining the house.

In-between she'd do all the other jobs that needed doing – the shopping, the cleaning, the laundry. My older brothers would look after themselves, but my mother was like a machine, working 24 hours a day it seemed. She was a remarkable woman, who had come from little, earned a great deal, lost it all and then set about rebuilding it again, both for herself and for her children. She was born and brought up in a village and although my father's father was a doctor, her father was a farmer and she had little education growing up and none of the luxuries of the more educated and affluent.

Her persona was larger than life and everybody loved her. She was pretty, fair, charismatic and I always felt that she glowed with a special aura. I'm not the only one; everybody who met her says the same. She and my father were introduced by relatives whilst he was a police inspector working in the area where she lived. They fell in love and got married, despite the difference in their status. It was my father who educated her. He felt uneasy that, despite her natural self-assurance, his wife was unable to converse on the same level as the memsahibs whose husbands held senior roles in the police force and with whom he had to mix with socially and professionally. He paid for a tutor and my mother discovered a passion for education and self-improvement that remained with her throughout her life. It was my father's ambition that she should educate village children alongside the English ladies and, having realised how learning could transform the fortunes of village children, she threw herself into it willingly and became a great teacher in her own right.

Later on, in England, she lived with me for some years before moving out to her own flat in Southall because she wanted independence. It was not long before her popularity grew. All the local ladies began to visit her to sit and listen to her stories as well as her advice. She became quite a matchmaker too. As I said, she was irrepressible and wanted to be involved with everything and everyone.

During my childhood, it was her determination that helped us survive. She was extremely resourceful – she had to be. As a single parent and a refugee, she had eight children to raise and educate. When we needed new clothes, she would go to better-off people and ask for their children's cast-off clothing. My mother was very strict about our education and wouldn't let us get jobs until we had finished studying. We all made sacrifices and helped out where we could. Exams cost money, so whoever had the best chance to pass would take the exam – "OK, I'll skip a year. You go." That way we all got our education, the best start in life that my mother could give us. It was one for all, and all for one.

If it wasn't for my mother's determination, strength and resilience, we would have probably ended up in an orphanage, or we could have just disappeared. Other mothers were forced to have their children work, either on food stalls or in shops or taking odd jobs to earn some extra money for the family. I was lucky to have a determined mother who did not allow any of us to work for a pittance and, in her mind, damage our future careers. "No matter how poor we are," she used to say, "you are going to study. You can be close to starving, but you will study. The only way we can get out of this mess is by education."

She was right. She made sure that we were all educated and, later on, were married into good families. Although we had become very poor, she made sure that our aspirations never became impoverished. She reminded us constantly of our family heritage and legacy – about our father and about his father who was a doctor. We came from educated, professional stock and she was determined that we would return there. Everyone in our wider family was struggling and none of us were able to help each other so we had to learn to help ourselves.

As we became older, my brothers left the family home one by one. One became a teacher far away on the north-west frontier in Assam, a godforsaken place. Five joined the army and became soldiers. This was seen as a good route out of poverty for young men and with their education in time they all became commissioned officers. As a commissioned officer they would earn 400 rupees a month, a good salary at that time. They lived in a mess so their living expenses were low and they were each able to send my mother 100 rupees a month. There was a commitment from all of us to support the family. It's a lesson I've taken into adulthood. As I became successful, I was able to help one of my brothers go to Canada to live, help him to settle, get his children educated and support them financially.

Every time a brother joined the army, life improved. The extra income reduced the strain on our resources and though we started poor, we became middle class. By the time I was 16, I was able to pester my mother for a bicycle, a luxury item at that time. It was the highlight of my life; I had got my very own set of wheels!

Eventually, my mother was rewarded for her hard work and sacrifice. In 1965, when I was 18, she was interviewed by the *Tribune* newspaper because she had five sons in the armed forces, three of whom were fighting on the border with Pakistan. No other mother in India could claim such an accolade, so the *Tribune* gave her the title of the 'Proudest Indian Mother'.

She was a remarkable woman and, although she is no longer with me, I am still proud of her. I have her picture next to me on my desk in my office because everything I have is because of her. Without her vision, her hard work, her commitment to our family and her support, somebody like me would not be where I am today.

She brought up eight children single-handedly, having lost her home and her husband and starting all over again in a strange place with so many liabilities. She discharged her duties remarkably well.

2. THE CAREFREE BOY GETS SORTED

A S A TEENAGER, I was spoilt and carefree. Being the youngest has its ups and downs in a large family – at times I felt that I was the last in line because there were so many people before me. But I was usually happy because I was well looked after by my mother, brothers and sister. Everyone around me gave me a lot of love and I was never short of anything.

Everything revolved around the family and we were very close-knit. In those days there was no television and little to do for entertainment. Besides, we couldn't afford many things – just having a good meal was an achievement for us. We always ate together and shared everything. Even after my brothers left home, they would come back on leave for a month each year and we would be as close as ever – eating together, still sharing our food; only now we could afford more and better food and eat what we wanted to, rather than what we could afford.

I was spoiled at home and I was spoiled at school. I went to my mother's primary school and, being a child of one of the teachers, the other children were scared of me and gave me respect that I had not really earned. To be honest, I received too much love and attention whilst I was growing up. Everything was made far too easy for me. I was lazy at school and not academically bright and when my mother put me into a good school I had to leave it because it was too much hard work and I couldn't keep up.

For me, life was easy and I was carefree. In the summer holidays we would go to my uncle's near Lucknow, where he had a farm and where I would play in the sugar cane fields with my cousins, most of whom are now scattered all over the world, in Australia, Canada, the United States and, of course, Great Britain.

I was far more interested in playing with friends than studying and had friend after friend after friend. I wanted nothing but friends and became very popular. I got on with people and I enjoyed their company. As I got older, I enjoyed going to the movies with friends or travelling to their villages outside Patiala to hang around the fields doing nothing in particular – often when I should have been in school.

I didn't like school. My aim was to find company and truancy became the order of the day. If we didn't skip school, we would just sit at the back of the class during lessons and chat or play games. The classrooms themselves were huge and classes consisted of anything between 70 and 100 children. It was too easy to go unnoticed, though I can see now that I didn't enjoy school because I made no effort to follow the teaching. You have to know what's going on to enjoy something, and I didn't have any idea what was going on. It's the same as if you go to an event and the people sitting at the front can hear everything clearly so they're enjoying it, but the people at the back are straining to hear, missing things and losing track. I sat at the back, chatted, played games and lost interest.

In a way, I was sorted, like a letter at the post office. There, the letters are sorted by area, whether Bromley, Sidcup, Reading, Slough or wherever. Similarly, in the classroom, the bright, industrious students will sit in the front row and pay attention to the teacher. The mediocre guys sit at the back. They don't want to sit and study; they want to chat and play games. If they like chasing girls, they're outside the girls' school. If they like hanging around in bars, they'll just go and sit in a bar. People get sorted according to their own desires and aspirations.

So I was sorted, just like that. I fell into bad company and became the most rebellious of my mother's children. As teenagers, we would ride motorbikes out to my friends' villages and hang around, again doing nothing. I would chase girls, get into fights and get up to no good. I was lucky not to get into trouble with the law because we sailed close to the wind at times.

I skipped two years of school because I was roaming around with friends rather than sitting in classes. Patiala was a large market town, a principality, and had everything a relatively modern city would have – a cinema, shops, bars, a station, colleges and a university. There were a lot of distractions and I completed my graduation from high school with a great deal of difficulty. I would just cram during the last month before an exam, scrape through, then spend the next nine months having a great time and playing around. Somehow I got through my exams and secured a place to do a one year pre-degree course at Mohindra College in Patiala in 1966.

I got through it, but still didn't have a taste for learning. At the end of the pre-university year, I tried to follow my brothers and join the Indian Army. With five brothers in the armed forces, I already felt part of a military family and joining them seemed a natural thing to do. Besides this, the army was the quickest and simplest route out of poverty for people like us. We didn't have the money to go to medical college or engineering college and study for six years for professional qualifications. The way I saw it, the army route was simple: you get selected, you get commissioned and then you're an officer living on free rations with good perks and salaries. You just pray that war never takes place – and 99 per cent of the time it doesn't with the Indian Army – and you enjoy a good life.

However, I was rejected. I tried twice as a teenager and was rejected both times. I was so disappointed then, but now I understand that this was the best thing to happen to me. My brothers were always on the move and sometimes they were on the battlefield. Their life was actually much harder than I imagined it when I was young – and when they finished their 20-year commissions they were back to square one, building a new life, whilst I had moved beyond them. So I have no regrets.

Needless to say, I'm proud of my brothers for what they achieved as soldiers. They built good careers and were very successful. They took courses and learned to maintain their self-discipline. They all rose to the rank of colonel in time and, en route, learned skills that set them apart from regular officers. For example, one became a German interpreter for the Army and later taught English to German students in Germany. Another became a Russian interpreter for the Indian Air Force. They were all exceptional in their own way. In the next generation, my sister's son also went into the Army and her daughter married a colonel. We became an army family. There was something in us as a family that made us all want to be better than the guy next door. There was sibling rivalry to be better than each other but this forced us all to go the extra mile.

After I was rejected from the army I suffered great disappointment, and opted to stay in education. Although I was a mediocre student and disliked lessons and learning, the most sensible thing to do was to stay on and do a degree. Even to get a clerical job in India, you needed a degree. With only a high school graduation, the best I could do would be to become some sort of *peon* – a low-level worker like a messenger in an office carrying files from A to B.

So I spent the next two years on a pre-degree course and the first year of a degree at Mohindra College. I was still very sociable and enjoyed meeting a much wider range of characters than I had mixed with at school and in the area where we lived.

I was having fun, but I was still lazy with my studies. My mother was not at all happy about my approach to education and would come to the college to check up on me. She'd demand of the staff "Where is he? Where is he?" and she wouldn't leave until they had confirmed that I was in class. This also happened when I was at university in Chandigarh. I hated her for spying on me, but she got what she wanted: I stayed in class and did my studies. I knew that if I skipped classes she would find out and shout and tell my big brothers what I'd done. Sometimes they'd just tell me off and sometimes they'd give me a good hiding. I was sensitive and even a small criticism was enough to hurt and embarrass me.

In 1968, when I was 21, I left Mohindra College for Government College in the new city of Chandigarh 40 miles away to take a BA degree in history, political science and English. My world was expanding and it felt like a natural progression to move away from Patiala, as my brothers had done. The town by now felt old and overcrowded; the streets and houses were untidy and the traffic was chaotic. By comparison, Chandigarh was a tidy, modern city – like Milton Keynes, say – with straight roads, new parks, fine houses and a modern, well-connected transport system. It was the first planned city to be built after independence and as all the affluent people began to move there, it now had the highest income per capita of any Indian city. The ambience was much better than Patiala and it felt like the place to be.

I chose my university subjects with a similar attitude to that of my school days – I wanted an easy, comfortable life. My reasoning was that they were not technical subjects and were easy by comparison with the sciences, mathematics or economics. It was the easiest course that I could do – and even then I barely graduated. I was still academically lazy.

Even today, after more than 40 years in the UK, I don't have great confidence with my English. I understand it perfectly and like to listen to the BBC World Service, where I've picked up lots of new words over the years that I would never have heard while growing up and learning English. However, although my understanding is good, when I speak I'm constantly thinking 'Am I speaking grammatically correctly or not?' I have to think of what I want to say first, mentally translate it from Punjabi and then speak.

Punjabi was the language that we spoke at home and in the street growing up, regardless of religion. In fact, it's now the second most spoken language in London after English, because of the Indian and Pakistani diaspora since the 1940s. Beyond Punjabi, which our mother tongue, we had to learn the national language, Hindi. We also had to learn English, which was the 'official language' and was used as a lingua franca because so many people in the south didn't learn Hindi.

There are big ethnic variations in India. The people in the south are the 'real' Indians – they are darker skinned and have not been disturbed by invaders like we had been in the north. We lived in areas that had been trade routes and borderlands for thousands of years, at least as far back as Alexander the Great. In fact, my family and I have Greek genes ourselves. I know this because I suffer from a form of anaemia called thalassemia, which is only found in the Mediterranean. When Alexander and his soldiers passed through India, many stayed and settled down in the area. It had taken months to get to India and you can imagine them thinking 'I'm not going back. I'll just find a girl and live here.'

So my ancestry goes back to Alexander and the Greek invaders. But there were also Persian invaders, Mongols, and we were close to the Silk Road that connected trade between Europe and and the Far East. We're much more culturally mixed than the south Indians, and fairer skinned.

We thus learnt several languages and grew up conscious of our mixed heritage. This understanding of different cultures has given me the confidence to have a truly international outlook as a businessman.

In 1971, I graduated from Government College in Chandigarh with a pass in history, political science and English. However, I was still just living day to day, having a good time, and not thinking about the future. I never planned for anything and hoped that everything would just fall into place. I had been rejected by the army and barely scraped through an easy degree. I was not at all visionary and had no idea what I really wanted to do with my life. I had been sorted.

This all changed when I came to England.

3. MY FATHER'S SHADOW

MY MOTHER WAS the biggest direct influence on my life but behind us all stood my father. Even though he was killed before I was born, his impact on my life has been enormous. Shaheed Nanak Singh was a man of exceptional ability, yet he was assassinated by religious fanatics because of his vehement opposition to the partition of India.

Growing up, I was very aware of my father and his achievements. It was his reputation, after all, that helped us get on the train from Gujranwala in August 1947 and then into our family home in Patiala. His influence on my mother was profound and she continued to impart his values of self-respect, discipline and family honour to us throughout her life.

My mother, along with my father's friends and relatives, have told me that he was the most charismatic and intelligent man that they ever came across. The son of a surgeon, he was raised in affluent surroundings and educated properly from his earliest days. He excelled, unlike me, and stood first in his class throughout his education. He was extremely bright and became a double graduate – first in science and then in law. On finishing his education, he joined the British police in India.

His sense of justice, strength of character and intelligence meant that he excelled as a police officer and received 29 certificates of commendation during his service. But his association with the police turned sour one day when he was asked to open fire on a group of unarmed protesters in Sargodha.

The group had gathered outside the commissioner's house to present a petition against the inhuman conditions in which the prisoners of the Indian national army were being held by the British. They were freedom fighters who were battling for independence from British rule. The years leading up to the end of the British Raj were full of unease and uncertainty. The British were nervous and wary of violence against their regime. The petition was refused and, despite several requests, the crowd would not leave. Instead, they became more agitated and a superintendent, an Englishman, ordered my father to disperse the protesters by opening fire on them. He refused. "Sir, they are unarmed," he said; "and though angry, they are not rioting. We should let them present the petition and then they'll go."

At this, the superintendent became more agitated and began to shout. "This is an order!" he exclaimed.

Calmly, my father removed his revolver and handed it to his superior. "Obey your own order," he told him.

Of course, the superintendent didn't.

My father's punishment was an official reprimand and a new posting to a tribal area at the Afghan border, a place no one wanted to be. Even today, the north-west frontier is a dangerous, lawless place. My father lasted for a year before he left the police altogether and returned home to

Rawalpindi, with the intention of setting himself up as a lawyer. His own father refused to fund this endeavour, and so my father found himself in Multan at the invitation of a friend – a Muslim aristocrat named Abdul Khan with whom he had studied law. It was Khan who helped my father establish himself as a lawyer.

Again, he became noted as a man of talent and conviction and his political principles developed. His experience with the British police had shown him that the British policy of divide and rule was now turning into divide and run away; they were turning their back on the consequences of the decisions they were making about independence. These consequences could be very dangerous for the country. The Indian independence movement was growing in strength and the campaign for a separate Islamic state was also gathering pace.

My father had a great sense of social justice and equality and he cared passionately about Indian unity and independence. India was a nation of diverse people and cultures who had lived together for centuries. My father campaigned vigorously against any kind of division, even persuading local Sikh leaders to abandon their demands for an independent Sikh state. He wrote papers and articles and gave provocative speeches at public meetings. "India is a motherland," he said, "not a property which can be divided so easily. We will never see peace if you create a country on the basis of hatred."

He warned the Muslim leaders that even if they got what they wanted, it would leave a legacy of division forever. "You are now united for the wrong cause," he told them. "Once you achieve your objective, you will turn on each other because there will be nothing for you to hold on to apart from your common desire to expel non-Muslims from your new country."

There was a lot of violence and rioting. Non-Muslims were being attacked and killed – even ahead of partition, there was a kind of ethnic cleansing going on. My father's speeches and articles made him a lot of enemies. On 5 March 1947, he heard that there were riots in Multan because students from the DAV School in the city were protesting against the partition of India and had been attacked by religious fanatics. My father went down to see if he could calm the situation, and was recognised by the leaders of the separatist mob. He was attacked and killed. He lost his life for the unity of India.

My father was right. The British had no idea what they were doing or what the consequences of their actions would be. They made the decision to split a nation that had existed for centuries in a matter of days, with no plebiscite, referendum or thought for the long-term implications. India and Pakistan have experienced 66 years of conflict and rivalry since that day – they have even become nuclear rivals. The consequences are also being felt in Britain where immigrant communities from India and Pakistan continue to live separately and often in conflict with each other. This is why I started the Pakistan, India and UK Friendship Forum – to reunite the communities in a new country where their historic separation should be irrelevant, since we now have one country and queen and, as a result, have become one.

The British simply did not understand India. They didn't understand that by playing into the hands of the Muslim majority in the north they were creating violent upheaval. It's estimated that up to a million people may have been killed during the turmoil of partition and around 14.5 million were displaced from their homes in the months following partition alone. Some 25 million in total have made the journey either way across the border since 1947.

My family were among the 7.5 million Sikhs and Hindus who travelled to the new Indian state of East Punjab in 1947. Even though they were previously the minority in the region that was to become Pakistan, the Sikhs and Hindus were the more prosperous and socially successful people; if they had not been, they would not have been expelled, but kept on to do the menial jobs where they would have been treated as second-class citizens. Instead, there was carnage.

India itself became calm quite quickly – after all, there was no expulsion of Muslims from India, as India chose to remain a secular nation. On the other hand, Pakistan has continued to experience violent upheaval through to today. As my father predicted, the Muslims fought among themselves. Within a quarter of a century, east Pakistan had split away to become the separate state of Bangladesh. The joke is that today there are more Muslims in India than there are in Pakistan. What was the point?

The biggest mistake was creating a country along religious lines. As soon as you allow religion to become the dominant political force, you have problems. Leaders are no longer selected on merit, but according to their religious status. Social advancement is the same. A country like this can't develop politically or economically, but will be beset by problems.

Though religion is very important in India, it is a secular and democratic nation. We were never given a high dose of religion when I was growing up – I had Hindu friends, Sikh friends, Christian friends, Muslim friends, and I considered them equals. We were all very anti-Pakistan, though, because of what had happened to our families and our society and because some of us, for example, had friends or relatives involved in military conflict with our Islamic neighbour.

Even though there were more Muslims in India than in Pakistan, there was little trouble in India. The Muslims in India didn't play the religious card; they were just like the rest of us and largely kept to themselves. Mostly they were shopkeepers and we would buy meat from them or go to cafés run by them. There were no problems. Besides, I was more interested in having a good time growing up – the problems with partition and Pakistan seemed a distant thing to me then and had little impact on my day-to-day life.

Even at 23, when I graduated from Government College in Chandigarh, I was still immature and naïve about the world. Having failed to get into the army and having little clear idea about what to do with my life in India, I decided to go to England instead, where I had a brother who was teaching. I would stay with him, do a law degree and live a prosperous and successful life in England; or I would return to India armed with a prestigious English law degree that would open the door to a wealthy life and high status. It all seemed so simple to me.

PART II.
GETTING STARTED

From frying chicken to my first business

4. WELCOME TO ENGLAND

ENGLAND WAS A total culture shock for me. I arrived on 22 May 1971 to study law. My aim was to do the bar-at-law exam and become a barrister, then return to India to practise, with the prestige of a British legal qualification. The same qualification in India would have taken three years to achieve, as opposed to two in the UK, so I was looking for a shortcut as usual. But the law changed that year so that overseas students like me could only qualify for a grant if they had already been living here for three years.

I simply couldn't afford to fund myself and I couldn't get a position with any firms that would sponsor me, so I had to change my plan. Life in England was a complete surprise to me. My idea of England had come from films and I believed money grew on trees and the streets were paved with gold. I imagined that I'd be living an easy life, earning well, spending money and enjoying myself. Nothing could have been further from the truth.

I came to live with my older brother Pritam and his family in Thornton Heath in southeast London. He was a teacher and had come to England via Tanzania in 1964. He had his own house, a wife and two children and I assumed his life was easy. I had no idea how he was struggling or that he also worked as a driving instructor to supplement his income. He would warn me: "Don't come. It's very tough." But I thought that he was just jealous and didn't want me to have a good time like I was sure he was having.

When I arrived, I realised how wrong I was.

I underwent a seismic change in my thinking. My survival in a new place that owed me no favours depended on it. My attitude, my outlook, my whole personality changed when I came to the UK. It dawned on me that I would genuinely have to fend for myself and I had no relevant education, no workplace experience, no financial help and no track record to ease the way for me. Although my brother and sister-in-law were very supportive during my first three months, I couldn't depend on them for ever. Nevertheless, they allowed me to sleep in a sleeping bag on their living room floor during those early months while I looked for work.

It was dispiriting. Everywhere I applied for a job, I heard the same thing: "Have you got experience? Have you got this? Have you got that?" When I saw that nobody would just give me things, I became utterly dejected and decided to go back to India. I was desperate to have a life in the UK, but not that desperate – it's not as if I had nothing to go back to in India. I still had my mother there, a home, opportunities to earn a living. But in order to get back home, I needed to earn money for the fare and, besides, it would have been humiliating to return so soon.

People wouldn't even believe that I had been to England. "He just went to Bombay and back," they would laugh.

But I made the decision to return. I would earn enough for my fare home and to buy back the things I had sold to get to England, such as my motorbike. That would get me back to square one and I felt it was the least I should do. So I continued to look for work, but I found that I was penalised as an Asian immigrant. It felt as though I was starting from 15 points behind everyone else because I was not English, white and did not have the old schoolboy network to support me.

In the early 1970s, we Indians were just beginning to arrive in Britain and we were still few and far between. Consequently, we had no track record of success and people's opinions of us were coloured by the negative news and TV images they got from India, which was still dealing with the problems created by partition and the war with Pakistan. There was also the lingering imperial perception that Indians were not that clever.

It was a severe disadvantage and it wasn't until Idi Amin expelled the Asians from Uganda that this perception began slowly to change. Ugandan Asians, when they arrived, were educated, rich and articulate. Unlike other Indian and Pakistani immigrants, they had means and they started buying houses and shops, and starting new businesses. After this, Britain began to see Asians in a more realistic light.

For us, Britain started to become a land of opportunity. Asians started to come in big numbers. Indian restaurants, sari shops and grocery shops appeared to serve the emerging communities, and in some cities entire neighbourhoods began to be transformed by the colours, smells and sounds that we had brought with us from our homeland. Before this, Asians had just been labourers coming to work in factories in the Midlands or the North. Now we were professional – we were doctors, accountants, solicitors, as well as restaurateurs and shopkeepers. People began to take us seriously and give us respect.

But this had yet to happen when I arrived in 1971 and nobody would take me seriously. My colour, my language and my culture were all handicaps to me. I slowly began to realise that the only way to overcome these kinds of drawbacks was to work harder than my English counterparts. Many of us Asians came to this realisation quite naturally. If the competition worked five days a week, we worked six. If they worked six days, we worked seven. If they worked eight hours, we worked ten.

We had no choice. We knew that for our survival we had to give more and accept less. It was tough. But when you know nothing else, it becomes the norm – you accept it: "As an immigrant," you say to yourself, "this is what I have to do to survive."

Once again, I had been sorted. But this time it was in a hostile place with little support and opportunity and I finally changed. I always say that you get two chances in life to do well. Your first chance you get whilst you are in school, college or university. If you excel in education, you do very well, you get a good job and you progress in life. The second chance you get is with a job. If you do your job well, it doesn't matter so much about your education because your relevant experience is now limited to that particular job. Your knowledge is now tested on what you can do in that narrow sphere. Your employer doesn't care whether you know about anything else. They just need you to do your job and do it well.

I got my second chance when I came to England and realised: "I am nothing here." I had been a mediocre student and blown my chance in my studies. I couldn't get onto a law course because I didn't have the funds. I was sleeping in a sleeping bag on my brother's living room floor in a small house in southeast London wishing that I could go back home. It brought home a stark reality of life – that it didn't matter what I thought about anything. What mattered at this moment was what people thought of me.

This realisation that to be successful in the world you have to earn the respect and goodwill of others doesn't come to many people until they are 30, 40 or even 50. Some people don't get it at all. I was lucky – I arrived at this conclusion when I was 23. My early days in England taught me that respect was not a right, as I had always assumed, but a privilege that has to be earned. From that moment on, whatever I touched, whatever I did, whatever job I got, I gave it everything I could. I always put in more than the next guy so I would be noticed, respected and rewarded. After such a carefree youth, this was a dramatic change for me.

My first job in England was as a car cleaner with the Sutton Motor Company. They would import Simca cars made by Chrysler from France and my job was to de-wax them, clean them and tidy them up for sale. I often worked in the garage or on the street, whatever the weather permitted. After having so many aspirations to be a barrister and have a comfortable life, I found it embarrassing. My journey to work was also lengthy and complicated, involving either a long walk or a bus from Thornton Heath to Croydon, then a train from Croydon to Sutton. 'What is this?' I would ask myself. 'You came from such a good family. You had so much going on in your life. What are you doing here?' Cleaning cars in the street was demoralising, but it was the only job I could get and at least it was a job. I was earning money and I remembered my mother's words that we should never be ashamed of work, but we should be ashamed of our misdeeds.

One day, as I passed a row of shops on my walk home from Norbury Station to Thornton Heath, I noticed a sign in a window: "*Kentucky Fried Chicken – opening soon. Chefs required – no experience necessary. Apply within.*" I walked through the door and told them that I was ambitious and hardworking. I got the job. 'This is fantastic,' I thought. 'I'll be near home, I'll be working inside and there will be no element of the weather disturbing me. If nothing else, there will be plenty of chicken to eat and I'll be able to look after myself better.' I looked at the advantages and I said: 'This is it. I'll take it.'

Kentucky Fried Chicken had only recently entered the UK and was undergoing a big expansion in London and southeast England. It was a good opportunity for me to develop with the company as it grew. I trained as a chef and was paid 35 pence an hour. I wanted to make lots of money so I worked every hour under the sun. I would get up early in the morning so that when my brother and his family came down to breakfast, the living room was already clear for them and they could sit and watch television before they went to work or school. I would already be gone and I wouldn't get home until long after they had all gone to bed. I'd creep in quietly so as not to disturb them, climb into my sleeping bag and start again the next morning.

I must have done this for two or three months before I was able to move out and get a room of my own. I found a shared house in nearby Norwood for £2.50 a week. I remember it clearly – a terraced house with four or five floors and basement, all broken up into bedsits. It was a grotty place with people of all nationalities living under one roof. We never knew each other; we would just open the door and go straight to our rooms where we cooked, slept and washed. The only thing we shared were the toilets. We were all living on the breadline.

My culture shock continued here. I was still saving to go back to India, so I was spending as little money as I could. I rarely had a proper meal like I had back home. Instead, I lived on baked beans, bread, fried chicken and whatever else I could get cheaply. It was very basic, but I just wanted to save money for the flight home. I said to myself, 'OK, I'll stay here for six months and go back.' This was my hidden agenda and why I worked hard. My employers had no idea. It was hope that sustained me. In life, you always have to have a goal, an ambition or something in your imagination that drives you. This was my goal.

In the process of working like this, I became respected, liked, and was promoted. I never said no to any request at work and was determined not to antagonise my boss or cause him problems. I reasoned that the people at the top also needed someone at the bottom to support them. I saw it as my job to take the pressure off my boss, not to induce more pressure by being awkward. Whatever he said, I just accepted and got on with it. I was conscientious and trustworthy. From chef, I became an assistant manager – it was like breaking the sound barrier for me. I didn't have to wear chef's clothes and stay in the kitchen all the time. Now I was the front man, standing at the counter and taking orders in a decent suit and tie. I was on my way.

A year later, I became a store manager, and, 18 months after that, a district manager, with responsibility for ten stores across southeast London as the KFC chain grew. I had a company car, an expense account and lots of perks. 'Who wants to be a barrister?' I thought to myself. My promotions were fast because the company had just arrived in the UK and they were expanding quickly by opening lots of stores. They were looking for people that they could develop from scratch and I was amongst the first to join. It just happened, in a way. I worked hard and

I learnt quickly and, even though I had no knowledge of anything else, I knew everything about chicken. As I said before, the only thing that matters in the workplace is what you know about what you do – and I made sure I knew more about chicken than anyone else.

I watched and learnt day in, day out. With experience comes knowledge, with knowledge comes confidence and with confidence comes promotions. It was the same years later when I worked as a store manager for Dixons after returning from a disappointing attempt to relocate to Canada. During my interview I said, "Look, I don't have much knowledge of electronics or electrical goods. I only know about the television we use at home."

"Don't worry," my interviewer said. "Within three months you'll know more about the electrical products than the customer." He was right, and I went on to become Dixons' leading store manager in London.

Once I was working and earning money, I never resented my situation. If anything I was grateful, because I knew that I had come to the UK out of my own choice and I was surviving with my own resources. It was an opportunity for me to show people how hard I could work and how reliable I could be. I wanted to earn their respect, so I never resented the work or the low pay or the lack of good meals. I was learning something very important that I tell my own staff to this day: before you can do the big jobs, you have to master the small ones.

The only times I felt disappointed were when I was passed over for a promotion. I had worked hard, I had done everything right, but still they underestimated me. It's a fact of life, of course, and I knew that as an immigrant I was starting from a lower point. But I took it personally as it also meant that I would miss out on extra money. I carried on working hard and became even more determined to prove my worth to my employers. I had got a job that I never deserved or expected and I just wanted to make sure that I made a good impression so they wouldn't get rid of me.

I was learning business throughout my time at KFC. I was learning how to manage an operation and how to motivate staff. I discovered that running a business was about effectively managing the men and material at your disposal, and it was a valuable lesson to learn. I stayed with Kentucky Fried Chicken until I was made redundant in 1976. I had been there for nearly six years and risen from chef to district manager, earning £200 a week. I was now married and living in a house in Penge in southeast London that I had bought myself.

1976 was a big year. It was the year that everything happened.

5. GROWING UP

N 1976 I GOT married, bought my first house and lost my job to redundancy. I had been in the UK for nearly six years and worked my way up from nothing to a district manager on a good salary and improving prospects. I had been thinking for a while that it was time for me to get married. I was no spring chicken now and I had seen my older brothers marry and have their own families. It was something I also wanted, and with my career steadily improving and the prospect of further success ahead of me, I felt it was a natural progression. So in 1975, when I was 28, I had set the process in motion.

Indian marriages in those days were arranged, as they still are for many people; not forced, but arranged – it's important to make that distinction. In a way it's like an organ transplant: you want to create a good match. With a transplant, you match blood type and tissue type so that there's no rejection. This is the case with an arranged marriage, except that now you are matching social strata, levels of education, family background and upbringing, professional accomplishment and so on. You're doing everything you can to increase the possibility of putting a man and a woman together who will understand each other and enjoy a good rapport as husband and wife. A bride's family might ask, "Has this boy grown up in a law-abiding environment? Has he been to a good school or university? Does he have the means to support a family and keep our daughter in comfort?"

These are things that the families discuss. Using their wisdom, maturity and experience, they help their children make a good match. But even then, there is no certainty: the boy and girl must also be attracted to each other. However well two people match on paper, the most important thing is to feel good with someone and be proud to be with them when you are amongst other people. Every husband wants to show off his wife and every wife her husband – it's human nature. It's not just about physical attraction, either, but the compatibility of personalities beyond physical appeal. To put it crudely, when you are trying to sell a product, the first thing your customer will focus on is the appearance. Then the quality of the product takes over and people stop caring so much about the packaging. It's the quality that they appreciate.

In India, marriage was something of an industry in those days and people would advertise for compatible matches in newspaper matrimonial columns. Although I had grown up in poverty, I had come from a good family with strong values, I was educated and I was doing well in my profession. My mother and I both thought that I could make a good match for a nice girl.

The Indian community in the UK was still not well-established and those who had come over tended to be married couples or single men. It's changed enormously now, but in 1975 there were far fewer eligible young Indian women in the UK than young men who were looking for a partner. So I cast my eyes back home to India and went to stay with my brother Brijinder in Delhi, where we put adverts into the newspaper matrimonial columns. We contacted some other advertisers and some people contacted us and I saw a few girls looking for a husband, but nothing worked. I was ready to give up and go home when my brother remembered someone he had met. "We have some distant friends in Delhi and they have a daughter," he told me. "You should see her." So we made an appointment to meet her father, Group Captain J. S. Lamba of the Indian Air Force.

I met my future father-in-law on a golf course whilst he was playing a round. He was impressed by me, as he had been to the United States and seen huge KFC restaurants in person. He thought, 'This guy has come from England, from a good family, he's a district manager at KFC in charge of ten stores,' and he said, "OK, you can meet my daughter."

We arranged a meeting and I went to the family home where I met my wife, Renu, for the first time. We liked each other immediately and I was given an opportunity to go out with her with a chaperone. We were just like any courting couple – we'd go to bars and restaurants, visit friends together and take walks. Renu was beautiful, intelligent, educated and confident, and she had a great sense of humour. She had all the qualities I was looking for in a lifelong partner and I knew she was the right woman for me. I returned to England engaged, and over the course of the next year we corresponded and phoned each other weekly, even though international calls were very expensive in those days. She asked me questions about England, my job and my ambitions; we discussed what it would mean for her to move to England with me – she was well educated and came from a good family. We discussed our future prospects. Renu decided she was willing to make the step. We got married and before I knew it, she became my boss. We didn't meet in person again until a week before the wedding, with her friend in attendance as always.

During our year-long engagement, I bought my first house. After all, I didn't want to bring my new wife back to rented accommodation where the landlord could be screaming and shouting. My income had become respectable, I had savings and I was able to put down a ten per cent deposit and raise a mortgage for a three-bedroomed semi-detached family home in Penge, which I bought for £13,000. Whilst we lived there, I would always tell people that I lived in Beckenham, the next town, which was considered to be a better postcode. Even when asked my address, my desire to better myself came through.

Renu and I had a traditional Indian wedding in Delhi in August 1976 and a civil marriage at Bromley Registry Office a short time later so that we could get our British wedding certificate. We've been together for 37 years now and she has always supported and complemented me, wherever we have been and whatever my ambitions. My wife is an exceptional woman and she understands what is required to be successful. Quite simply, I really can't imagine being successful without Renu. I certainly wouldn't be the man I am today.

Renu herself was brought up with wealth and was educated at a convent school run by Irish nuns. She went through college and university, always excelling, and her education is far better than mine. Yet she is humble. After she came to England, she sold penny sweets shoulder to shoulder with me in my first sub-post office shop, in Sidcup. When I was setting up my freight-forwarding business, Sea Air & Land Forwarding, she was working for the Ministry of Defence and I asked her, "Will you be able to support me for six months whilst I get the business off the ground?"

and she replied "Yes." Renu understood that you can't earn money from day one with a new business and that it takes time to pay your bills. She had full faith in me.

Later on, when I started my second firm, Sun Mark (a marketing company), we had no one to look after our day-to-day sales or trademark registrations in the UK, EU and elsewhere, and Renu took it on. She also handled the wages for the few members of staff that we had, looked after major accounts that we exported for such as Cadbury, Nestlé and Unilever, dealt with important customers overseas and looked after the stock situation for various companies in the warehouse.

What's more, she raised our three daughters, had her own career and supported me in both my business and community lives. She has always been there, encouraging me, advising me, listening to my complaints, watching my back, checking the English in my speeches, never unfairly criticising or challenging my decisions and commitments unduly. I may look like the front man, but I always say that when you look from a distance at a flag on top of a building, you cannot see the wires that support the mast and allow the flag to stand.

In my life I have so many people who help me project myself publicly and without their help I would probably fall flat on my face. Renu has been my greatest support. Think of it another way: imagine a plane with one engine, and then a plane with two. The twin-engine plane will go further and faster. Renu and I are a partnership and we pull together in the same direction. We've come very far together in the 37 years since we married.

So I was married, had my first home and was enjoying a good career with a respectable salary. Then out of the blue I was made redundant by KFC because they sold their shops and turned the business into a franchise operation. My role was no longer needed and they let me go. I was stunned. This was a serious blow. Renu and I had to take what we could. She got a job as a clerical officer with the Inland Revenue and I found a role as a salesman for McCain Foods. I was still in the food business, but I hated it. I was cold calling at shops, travelling from place to place, and standing around waiting to be seen selling chips. I loathed it, but I stuck at it out of necessity for a couple of years whilst we planned our next move. During this time Renu became pregnant with our first child and we arranged for my mother to come from India and live with us.

Any thought of returning to India was now gone completely. I was married, with a home and a child on the way, building a foundation in Britain. I was aware that there were more opportunities for me to build my own life in Britain than there were in India, and I was feeling more British by the year. India was distant now, forgotten almost; it seemed to belong to another person entirely. No matter how difficult things got, Britain was my home.

There were two new arrivals in 1978 – my mother and my first daughter Reena, who was born in March. I was no longer the single guy with nothing to lose; I had family to take care of now and I made a big decision: I decided to do what every Indian was doing back then and bought a corner shop in Sidcup, with a sub-post office attached. Even though things were beginning to change, good jobs and promotions were still hard to come by for Asians in the UK. So we became independent businessmen and women; we ran our own shops and small businesses – we did what we could to make an independent income because we knew that we couldn't rely on others to give us a break. A shop was the perfect solution.

6. FIRST STEPS IN BUSINESS

MY FIRST THREE businesses were all local corner shops – a post office, an off-licence and a convenience store. In a way these were foolproof businesses because they came with accommodation and a ready flow of customers. They gave me income and properties that I could improve over time and sell at a profit. During my time at KFC, I'd learned about the logistics of running a business – the management of stock and materials, marketing, selling, cash flow, profit and loss and the importance of good customer service with attention to detail. I was confident in my ability to manage an operation and felt that whatever small shop I took on, I could make it work.

These were years of growth and development for me personally and as a businessman. I learnt more and more about the responsibilities and challenges of running a business and supporting a family. It wasn't all plain sailing, of course: I made mistakes and errors of judgement, including one enormous one that almost broke me. But I learned, and as a family we stuck together. I was no longer the carefree lazy boy of my childhood in India but a man taking responsibility for building a good life for myself, my wife, my child and my mother in the UK. It was hard work and I had learned not to be afraid of that. By the end of this chapter in my life I was ready to start my own venture from nothing and take a further step in the journey towards the man that I am today.

Our first shop was a newsagent with a sub-post office in a small strip of shops in Longlands Parade, Sidcup, Kent, a few miles east of where we had been living. I bought this with the proceeds of the sale of my house in Penge. We moved into the flat above the shop. Renu ran the post office and I managed the convenience shop in front. My mother took care of Reena while we worked downstairs. We all contributed to the running of the household and the family business.

Running a shop was hard work. Our opening hours were long, from early morning till late, and I was on my feet all day. In the evenings, I'd go to the cash and carry to pick up stock. I used to spend a portion of my evenings shifting heavy packages from my estate car to the shop and restocking shelves. At times it was mundane work and I would often find myself standing behind the counter waiting for customers with little to do because I'd already done the jobs that needed doing. At other times we were overwhelmed: on Tuesdays and Thursdays, for example, we needed extra help in the post office to cope with the rush for paying out child benefits and pensions. I have no idea how we did it all. I wouldn't be able to run a shop now – it's far too draining.

But I was gaining experience, knowledge and the confidence to run my own business without any support systems. We put a lot of effort into improving each of the three shops that we ran in subsequent years; we always built them up. We refurbished the interiors, increased the opening hours, bought a better quality of stock and extended the lines in the shops to pull in more customers. We bought the Sidcup shop for £30,000 in 1978 and sold it for £50,000 just two years later. Running the shops was definitely worth the investment of time and effort. Plus, as I have said, it was a convenient arrangement for us in those days, as it left us the masters of our own destiny.

Nevertheless, I was not very comfortable, as post offices were common targets for robberies. I was always nervous that the post office might be robbed when I was not on the premises and my wife, child and my elderly mother would be alone and unable to defend themselves. At times there was a lot of money in the shop, sometimes as much as £70,000 in pension money. It is worth remembering that this was a time when an average three-bedroom house would cost just £13,000 or £14,000. The post office was too great a risk and played on my nerves constantly; and I have never been a risk-taker.

After close to two years in 1980, we sold the post office and bought an off-licence a few miles away in St Paul's Cray, between Sidcup and Orpington. I knew that tobacco and alcohol would always sell, and we also stocked newspapers, sweets etc. I had no doubts about my ability to make an income. However, the off-licence was on a large council-owned housing estate and it proved to be quite tough. I still worked very long hours, starting early in the morning and finishing late seven days a week. I felt no more secure than I had at the post office. Off-licences too were robbery targets and my familiar fears remained.

I became fed up with the constant anxiety playing on my mind and the limited time I had to spend with my growing family. I was looking for a way out.

I allowed myself to be talked into what was comfortably the worst decision of my life.

My brother Rupinder was now living in Canada and working as a civil engineer in Calgary, Alberta. He'd been nagging at me for some time to relocate to Canada where he said that life was wonderful. "Oh, what a great country," he'd say. "The economy is booming and it's a lovely atmosphere. You should come here and we'll be together again."

This was something of a dream which I didn't really consider seriously until two of my other brothers in India, who had left the army, proposed a joint venture in Canada. Both wanted to strike out overseas and would have come to the UK but immigration was suspended at the time. We all talked and came to the conclusion that Canada would offer a great opportunity for us to be together again whilst running a family business. I thought that if I sold everything, we would have a good amount of capital and would be able to finance a good-sized business in Canada and run it together.

Our idea was to buy a motel which, like a shop, would provide a family home and a steady stream of customers. I imagined that, with the responsibilities split between three brothers and our wives, it would also be less demanding on my time than a shop, and would afford me the chance to spend more time with my growing family. I viewed this also as a foolproof business. Canada is a huge country and people travel great distances by car so I imagined that a well-run motel in the right location would always get business. I was confident that if we found the right motel we could make it work. I caved in and made the decision to emigrate for a second time.

We set the move in motion quickly in late 1980. Renu was pregnant with our second child, Amita, and the Canadian High Commission in the UK was keen that she had the child in Canada rather than the UK. We were under pressure to move fast, and we did. We put the off-licence up for sale, sorted out the paperwork and moved to Canada. Rupinder was based in Calgary but we decided to head straight for Toronto, Canada's largest city, where I felt the chances of finding a profitable business would be greater. We moved with £100,000, the proceeds from the sale of my properties. I thought this would be enough but it wasn't.

Truthfully, it takes four to five years to establish oneself in a new country and £100,000 was peanuts for what I wanted to achieve. We lasted just a year. Rupinder's account of the booming Canadian economy proved false. In fact, we moved to Toronto in the midst of a deep recession. Interest rates were very high and the minimum lending rate was 20 per cent. What could one buy when the interest rate was that high? The news was full of businesses closing and people losing their jobs and homes. Our plan for Renu to find a government job that would provide security and flexibility was also a non-starter because the government was not employing people unless they were Canadian citizens. The best place we could find to live on our small budget was a basement apartment in the poor end of town that was infested with cockroaches and rats. There was absolutely no prospect of me buying the motel that I had dreamed of, not least because my brothers abandoned their plan to come to Canada after visiting and seeing what the conditions were like.

We were hamstrung. We had no chance. It was an awful and terrible mistake during a period of my life that I would like to forget. I had simply made a quick move out of desperation. If I had done my research, I would never have gone there. It was my first and so far my only real failure. This error of judgement was big because it affected everyone around me. I became very low but I had the strength of mind to realise that the best course of action would be for us to return to the UK and to what we knew. We had lost half of our capital but £50,000 would still be enough to re-establish ourselves in England where I was familiar with the system.

The only light during this dark and difficult period was the birth of my second daughter, Amita, in June 1981. Rather than being born in Canada she entered the world in the United States, in Akron, Ohio. We travelled there for her birth at the invitation of Renu's uncle, Jitender, who was a radiologist at the hospital where Renu gave birth and where he made sure that mother and daughter were given the best care possible. Like all of my daughters, Amita has grown into a beautiful, intelligent young woman of whom I am extremely proud. In fact, she has become a doctor herself, continuing a family tradition that includes her great uncle on Renu's side of the family and her great grandfather on mine.

In the summer of 1981 we came back to London – Renu, Reena, Amita and I. My mother had not accompanied us to Canada but had returned to India to live with my brother Devinder. We had £50,000 and nowhere to live. A friend of mine, Ishwer, put us up at his home in Heston in Middlesex whilst we got back on our feet.

My children slept on the settee and Renu and I slept on the living-room floor. I was back on the floor again, just as I had been when I first came to the UK. Only now, it wasn't just myself that I had to support but a growing family. This time, I had knowledge and confidence in my ability to start again. This period in my life was a great test of my character and I came through it. In 1971, during my first few months in London, I had experienced a huge change in my thinking. This too was a turning point and it was just as significant, if not so dramatic. My Canadian experience humbled me. I was determined that I would never make a decision out of desperation again.

We lived with Ishwer for several months whilst I looked for a business. I decided to settle for another convenience shop because I understood them and knew how to make them work. But this time I'd use better judgement in my choice of shop. I found a very rundown shop with a flat above it in Harrow in northwest London, directly opposite the Harrow and Wealdstone railway station. It was perfect. It had been neglected and was in dire need of improvement. The potential for high footfall was considerable and I knew I could improve the property and the shop and turn it into a goldmine. I also made sure to buy the freehold rather than simply the leasehold. I'd realised there was potential in property but it depended on having complete ownership. I'd never bother with leases again.

We relocated to west London, where we remain today. We started again. It was hard work. The shop, called Rolf's, had been owned by an elderly lady and was in a dilapidated state. Her husband had died and she had lost interest in the business. It was barely ticking over when I bought it. We moved in during the winter of 1981 and spent the winter gutting the shop completely and cleaning it from top to bottom. We removed all the furniture and carpets from the flat upstairs and all the shelving and fittings from the shop below. It was a nightmare. There was no heating and it was freezing cold. We all fell ill. But we kept going. We redecorated the flat and refurbished the shop, refitting the interior and putting a new aluminium front on the shop which made it look brighter and more welcoming.

I used the knowledge I had built up through running small shops before and applied it to maximise the potential of the business. Rolf's was a typical newsagent and convenience store. However, we changed the suppliers, added new lines and increased the opening hours until

8pm. My wife and I ran the shop between us. By now, my mother had moved back to England and looked after Reena and Amita while we worked. The location, just opposite the railway station, was excellent and we started picking up passing trade that the shop had previously missed out on because it had looked so neglected and unwelcoming. Once again, we worked hard, from 6 in the morning until 8 at night, seven days a week, but we made the shop a success.

We carried on like this for two years, but, as before, I couldn't help feeling that I was missing out on spending time with my family. We were also asking a lot of my mother, who was over 70 now, and no longer had the energy to look after two lively young children. I needed a solution, something that would enable us to benefit from the capital that we had worked so hard to build up, whilst reducing our working hours so we could spend more time together.

I weighed up my options and thought about how I could use the shop to earn a partial income while I took on a full-time job with standard working hours. I leased the shop and received a £30,000 goodwill payment plus £10,000 a year rent for a 15-year lease. We got a mortgage and bought a four-bedroomed semi-detached family home in Kenton, also in west London, for £50,000. Once we moved out of the flat above the shop, we converted it into offices and I leased those to a business for £7,000 a year. So I was making £17,000 a year from the shop, which in 1983 was a good salary in its own right. I went back to working for someone else for the first time in five years. I got a job as a trainee manager in Currys, the electrical retailer, in their Wood Green store in London. Another chapter of my life began.

7. BACK TO WORK

I STARTED WORK as a manager for Currys at their Wood Green store in 1983. My previous sales and managerial experience with KFC, McCain and with my own businesses stood me in good stead. Even though I knew nothing about electronics, it didn't matter. I'd demonstrated that I could learn quickly. And as I said earlier, if you're dedicated you will almost always know more than the customer about the product within a few months.

Life was going well. I was no longer working in the evenings or on Sundays and was able to spend much more time with my family. The income from the shop in Harrow and Wealdstone kept coming and Renu got a good job at the Naval Secretariat in the Admiralty at the Ministry of Defence. We felt secure. For the first time in many years we had real quality time together as a family. We took holidays; we started exploring the UK. We were happy.

I was successful at work. Currys was taken over by Dixons in 1984 and I was promoted to manager of the Cheapside store in the City. It was a prestigious position within the company and I did well. I produced outstanding results and profits for the company and became Dixons' top store manager. We should have been flying; but things are rarely as you wish them to be.

News came from India that my brother Brijinder had died. He was just two years older than me and we had always been close. It was Brijinder who had helped me find Renu when I was seeking a wife. His death was a terrible blow and sat heavily on me for a very long time. But I coped. I had to. I had obligations to my family and my employer.

However, I began to experience frustrations at work. My area manager was a man who seemed to lack empathy and treated me poorly. Even though I was the company's top store manager, he continually undermined me and made my life difficult. I was doing everything right but whenever there was a shortage of staff elsewhere, he would take my staff, upsetting the running of my store. I felt he was just thinking, 'This guy is desperate. He's not going to argue and he's not going to give me lip and cause trouble.'

He knew I would carry on regardless and continue to make things work. Sometimes, if you are successful, people take advantage of you. It is the price you pay for being capable; if you're not successful, people don't ask you for help. They only ask when they know you can cope – even if it means you are continually working at a disadvantage. So, in a way, my success became my downfall. I was losing my sales staff. I even lost my assistant manager. Whenever I built a good team and got my staff working well, they were taken away from me. I felt as though I was being picked on for being very good at what I was doing and I couldn't understand why.

I started to struggle and became very unhappy. One day, when I felt I'd had enough, I went to the Dixons head office to confront my boss.

"Are you happy with my performance?" I asked.

"Yes. Excellent," he replied.

"So I'm your number-one manager? I produce the maximum sales and maximum profit?"

Again, he agreed.

"Then why do you always take my staff?" I demanded. "I come to work and you just upset my schemes. You take my staff, you increase my workload, you scupper whatever plans I have for the day. You prevent me from increasing my sales."

He was rude to me in return and refused to listen or sympathise. In the end he said, "Do you know whose name is outside the shop?"

"Dixons," I said.

"Exactly," he replied. "So you'll do whatever Dixons tells you to do. End of story."

I walked away in tears. I felt undervalued and undermined and I was starting to feel even more unhappy. But worse was to come. One of my daughters fell ill with a serious condition that required regular hospital treatment during the day. I would leave at lunchtime, collect her from school and drive to hospital for treatment, back to school then race back to work late afternoon. Apart from the worry about my daughter's health, I was also concerned about my performance at work. I was the manager with responsibilities and obligations and I couldn't have people saying, "This guy, he's taking more than an hour for lunch. He's taking the mickey." I couldn't allow myself to be anything other than the number-one store manager. Anything less would be a failure to me. I was putting myself under a lot of pressure to remain at the top.

Life had become completely regimented. Renu left for work early in the morning and I would get the children ready and drop them at school, then jump on the train straight to work. I was skipping breakfast and frequently lunch too. I was neglecting myself and constantly felt tired and stressed. Without noticing what was happening, I slipped into depression and began to unravel.

One day I made a mistake at work. It was a small error of judgment, really, but it had a terrible effect on me. I had sold a lot of electrical equipment to a customer and he returned a few days later with a hi-fi. It was covered in scratches, one or two bits were broken and it had obviously been used. But he claimed that it was like this when he took it out of the packaging and demanded a refund.

"You can't have a refund, but I will get it fixed for you," I explained. "You've used it and it is still under guarantee."

"I want a refund," he insisted.

"But it's scratched, it's broken," I pointed out. "You can't have a refund if it's been used. That's company policy."

"Right, I'm going to call your head office and complain that you're refusing me a refund for damaged goods."

I was so anxious about the involvement of head office that I caved in and gave him the money. It was the wrong thing to do, but I just wanted the problem to go away. That night, on the train home, I felt my body tensing up. My chest became very tight and I felt that both my mind and body were out of control. I was terrified. I thought I was about to have a heart attack. I was so tired and so stressed by the weight of all that I'd been carrying since my brother's death that I was breaking down. It was too much. I had pushed myself too hard for too long and I plunged deeply into depression and anxiety.

The feeling that I had failed in my obligations and duty to my family and my employer persisted for a long time. I lost the self-respect that I had worked so hard to earn and I felt that others no longer respected me either. It was crushing my ego. I struggled to sleep. I struggled to get up in the morning. I struggled to make decisions and work effectively. It was a terrible time. I was worn out. I had to tell my boss that I was suffering from nervous exhaustion. He was as unsympathetic as ever. I felt trapped. I knew I had to escape but I didn't know how. I was at my weakest point and I remained there for a long time.

My depression affected me very badly and it took me years to recover properly. Depression occurs when your mind and your body are out of synch with each other. My body was exhausted but my mind was still telling me to work hard, to drive myself and to fulfil all of my obligations to everyone. It was too much for my body to handle at that point and I didn't realise it soon enough. I started to feel like I was failing. I felt weak, useless, a failure and I started to have very dark thoughts.

I had to wrestle with myself and learn to block out these thoughts. I had to reassure myself constantly – "I'll be alright. I'll be alright." It's very confusing when you find that you can't do the things you were able to do just a short time ago, things that you simply took for granted. I began to think that perhaps I was losing my mind but it was all in my imagination; my brain was fine. I just had to accept the reality of my situation – that I had pushed myself too hard and that I needed to recover physically before I could return to my former self mentally. I was not even 40. I was still young and energetic but had to accept that it would take time for me to recover and recover I would.

This is the secret to recovering from depression. You have to accept your circumstances and live with what you have now, not what you had six months or a year ago. If you lose your legs in an accident, you cannot dream of living as if you still had legs. You must live in the present, accept the reality and learn to live with that. Then you will recover from the depression that comes with the loss of your former self and you will become healthy again.

I learned this eventually. However, my confidence had taken an enormous blow and I was at a very weak point for a long time. I was also trapped in a working environment which I wanted to escape from. In spite of my hard work and success, I was not being properly recognised or rewarded for my achievements at Dixons. I felt undervalued and the company was not giving me a chance to shine or feel good about what I was achieving. I needed a way out. And I found it, thanks to a chance meeting with a friend at a party in 1985.

My friend was an expert in customs clearance and had set up a customs brokerage through which he took care of the tariffs, duties and taxes for businesses that were importing goods into the UK.

I thought about my job at Dixons and said, "You know, a lot of people come from Africa and the Middle East to buy electrical goods and then ship them back home. It's difficult for them to get things like televisions and microwaves in their own countries and they come here to buy them and send them home as unaccompanied baggage. A lot of items get damaged or broken in transit because they're not packed properly and there's no one really taking care of the delivery at the other end. I think there's an opportunity there."

My friend asked questions and thought it over for a moment. Then he said, "Come and join me. You can do the export and I can do the import." So we struck a deal and I took my first steps towards the businesses I run today. In fact, I started my first business – Sea Air & Land Forwarding

– whilst I was depressed. I feel that finally doing something completely for myself helped me to pull me away from my dark thoughts and return to health.

*   *   *   *

A man is made of his circumstances. The chance discussion with a friend at a party was the circumstance that led me to where I am today. But it was far from a trouble-free beginning.

By 1985 I had been in England for 14 years. I was married and had two daughters. I had owned and run three small businesses. I had made good decisions and bad ones, made money and lost money. I had reached the glass ceiling working for other people and felt frustrated by a corporate culture that seemed to stifle merit rather than reward it. It had been a risk leaving India and I arrived in England with nothing but the values instilled in me by my mother and my faith. These have helped me to survive and even thrive at times.

But I felt there was so much more that I could achieve. I was restless, frustrated and ambitious. Now I took another calculated risk and embarked on yet another long and difficult journey, one that would ultimately give me everything I wanted.

My friend and I turned to a mutual friend to help us draw up an agreement about the business that we had discussed at a party. I was to be his employee and set up a new export side to his existing customs clearance business. In return, I would receive a commission of 40 per cent of whatever profit I generated annually from the export business on top of a £100 per week basic salary to cover my day-to-day costs. I would also be given a company car. My arm of the business would have to shoulder half of the premises costs of the whole business – warehouse rental, utilities, and so on.

I agreed because I could see that this was a real opportunity to escape from the circumstances that had led to my depression and it was a chance to work with a high degree of independence again. Though technically an employee, I would effectively be working for myself and taking responsibility for an operation that had a lot more potential to grow than a local shop.

I was organised, hardworking and determined to provide the best service I could. Furthermore, rather than simply improving a business that had already been built by someone else, I would be able to build an operation from the ground up and create the kind of business that reflected my values and principles in every area of operation. Even though freight-forwarding was a new field for me, I was sure I could set up the export arm properly and make it work.

Because of my recent experience, it made sense to start off with electrical goods. If Dixons were attracting overseas buyers, then I knew that other electrical retailers would be too. Using the cold-calling experience I had gained as a salesman for McCain, I trawled the electrical shops on Tottenham Court Road and Edgware Road in London. I met with shop owners, talked to them about their customers and explained the service I could offer. I began to pick up business.

From the start, I paid great attention to detail and made sure I provided a high standard of service for a good price. I ensured all the goods were packed properly with the right materials and I followed up every delivery to check that the customer had received their TV, video or music centre intact at the other end. I had long learnt that my reputation depended on the quality of service I provided, so I did all I could to make sure my name was as good as it could be.

Business snowballed and my efforts quadrupled the overall business revenue. After a year, I looked forward to receiving my commission of 40 per cent of the profit produced by my hard work. But it didn't come. My friend realised that I was desperate to make things work because I had a family to care for, commitments to honour and a reputation to build. He must have also reasoned that I wouldn't leave whatever pressure he put me under – after all, he knew at the outset that I was at a very low point in my life and seeking an escape from stressful circumstances.

"We'll sort out the profit payment next year," he told me. "This isn't something we can divide up and share out overnight. It's not like a fruit and veg business where you buy your stock in the morning, sell it during the day and cash up in the evening. This is an investment. Besides, you don't need the money right now – you have rental income coming in from your property. It'll be three years before you start seeing any money."

Though his argument about investing in growth wasn't entirely unfair, I felt that he was taking advantage of me. He hadn't even bought me a pair of weighing scales to weigh goods or provided me with the company car he had promised, let alone paid me my commission. I wrote him a letter explaining what I'd done to build up a new arm to his business that had quadrupled his revenue. I pointed out how much profit he was making now and reminded him of our agreement. I told him that if he wasn't going to stick to our contract, then I had no incentive to work for him any longer and I may as well set up my own operation where I could keep all of the profits for myself.

I was still fragile from my depression and full of self-doubt but I knew that the business had come about through my efforts. I felt deeply insulted and undervalued once again. I decided to give my friend one more chance to honour our agreement and called a meeting with the mutual friend who had helped us draw up our contract in the first place.

Despite the fact that we had made a gentlemen's agreement on a handshake, I had insisted on having the terms written down for a simple reason: my childhood in India had taught me to be streetwise and not to take people at face value. I knew that when people have nothing to lose at the outset of any venture they are all together but when money comes into the scenario, they change. I was not naïve. I knew that if the business became successful, it was likely that there would be disputes. There almost always are.

I held the meeting in the hope that our mutual friend would take a neutral view and point out to my employer that he had to honour the deal we had struck and pay me the commission that was due in light of my success with the export side of the operation. But, like many people afraid of displeasing someone in a position of power, he sided with the owner of the company and not me, the employee.

"It's agreed that you're a good manager," he said, "but the business is coming in because of the name of the company."

Given that both men knew I was struggling financially with all of my responsibilities, it was a heartless thing to say. I was incensed but I kept my counsel and thought about what to do next. I spoke to some of my customers. I asked them what they would do if I were to leave and set up my own business. "We're very happy," they said. "We only do business with you. We don't even know this other guy."

My mind was almost made up. I talked to my accountant to find out what my options were legally and what chance there was of receiving the commission money that I had been promised. He looked at the books and explained that the way the company accounts were being managed meant that the money for my commission just wasn't there. "You might as well leave," he said. So I did. I could have carried on in the hope that I would see the fruits of my labour eventually, as I'm not one to give up easily. However, I was not prepared to accept injustice once again.

It had been 18 months since we started working together and we had been in dispute for six of those. Despite my success, I had been treated as though my efforts counted for nothing at all. I can only think my former friend and employer must have lacked vision. I was building a profitable business for him, sharing half his premises costs and he could have kept 60 per cent of the profit I made for him without doing a thing. When a bad employer doesn't look after his staff, the staff either go and work for the competition or start their own business and become the competition.

As I said, a man is made of his circumstances. I worked very hard for various companies, but my success always became my downfall because of other people's envy, prejudice and reluctance to give credit where it was due. By now, though, I had developed good judgement and trusted my ability to make good business decisions and deliver what I promised. I had proven that I could build a business of this kind from nothing and make it work. I already had the trust of customers. My friend thought I didn't have the resources to leave and set up on my own, but he was wrong.

I may not have had much in the way of capital but I had knowledge, experience and confidence. Like others, he underestimated me and I proved him mistaken. I feel no bitterness, though. Our dispute spurred me to start my own ventures, and they have given me so much. So there was a silver lining. My accountant has since said, "He did you a favour. Had he paid you the commission, you wouldn't have progressed to where you are today."

It was a blessing in disguise. Though I had worried for months, leaving my friend and his business was an easy thing to do in the end. I realised that the only way out for me – to earn the respect I craved from others and fully restore my own self-esteem – would be to start my own business and become my own boss once again.

'You've got to do your own thing,' I told myself. So I did.

My brothers, sister and me outside our family home in Patiala in 1958. From left to right, Brijinder, me, Devinder and Kulvinder.

Me, aged 20 in 1967, at Mahendra College, Patiala, wearing my National Cadet Corps uniform. Although I joined the cadets and wanted to follow in my brothers' footsteps, I was not accepted by the Indian Army.

The family home in Gujranwala where I was born and spent the first few weeks of my life before our evacuation to Ferozepur in 1947.

My mother and father on their wedding day in Rawalpindi in 1931.

My father and mother with their first four children in 1940. My sister is in my mother's lap.

Playing with an early home computer in Dixons in Cheapside, 1984. I became the company's leading store manager during my two years with the firm.

With the Kentucky Fried Chicken company car outside my home in Downs Road, Beckenham, Kent, 1974. I was district manager, with responsibility for ten stores around southeast London until 1976.

On my wedding day with Renu, my new bride, in September 1976. Renu
has been a great support to me for almost 40 years.

With my family in the back garden of our first house, Oak Grove Road, London in 1981. I am standing on the far left with my late brother, Pritam, who helped me settle in the UK. My daughter Reena is at the very front in the arms of my nephew Pritinder. My mother is in the middle in the green suit with her two daughters-in-law beside her: my sister-in-law, Noni, on her right and Renu on her left. Renu's mother, Nilima, is beside her on the far right. At the rear of the photo Mr Lamba is carrying my youngest daughter, Amita, now a doctor.

Standing proudly at Sun Mark's centre of operations in Greenford. This shot was taken when I won the Institute of Directors' Director of the Year for Large Business in London and South East Region 2012.

PART III.
MAKING MY MARK

From freight-forwarding to Buckingham Palace

8. A BRAND NEW VENTURE

I STARTED SEA Air & Land Forwarding in August 1987 with a £40 typewriter, £2 capital and a table given to me by my first customer, a photocopier dealer who had bought himself a new desk. My first premises – if I can call it that – was a storage space rented from Abbey Self Storage in Hayes for £120 a month. We still had the income from our rented shop in Harrow, and Renu was earning money from her job with the civil service. I knew that it would take a while for my business to start earning me a proper income and Renu had agreed to support me for the first six months or however long it took for me to stand on my feet.

I stuck with what I knew and used the connections I had built up over the previous 18 months, concentrating on shipping electrical goods overseas. I continued dealing with the retailers in Edgware Road and Tottenham Court Road and my customers also included wealthy individuals who had been happy with my services and had stayed loyal to me. They mostly came from oil-rich countries in West Africa like Nigeria and Ghana and travelled to London to buy the goods they couldn't get in their own countries from high-end stores like Harrods and John Lewis. They stayed with me because they trusted my service as one would trust a good doctor, accountant, solicitor or anyone who provides an important personal service. They knew that I would take care of their purchases to ensure that everything arrived safely at the final destination.

I also saved them money. There are two ways to transport luggage by air – you can take goods as accompanied baggage with you to the passenger check-in, which then get put onto the same plane. Or you can transport it as unaccompanied baggage by sending it via the cargo shed. It will travel separately and you can collect it from the cargo shed of the destination airport a day or two after you arrive at your destination.

Though travelling with accompanied baggage is more convenient, it's also a lot more expensive – perhaps even ten times as much. If you arrived at the airport with a large package – for example, a television or a microwave – you would be charged £10 a kilo in those days to send it through the passenger terminal. However, if it went via the cargo shed as unaccompanied baggage, it would only be £1 a kilo. This represented enormous savings, but it was a lot of extra hassle for passengers, who would have to employ an agent to book their luggage in as unaccompanied cargo and take care of the paperwork. Plus, if the baggage wasn't properly packed, it could get damaged or broken. Sometimes items went missing altogether if not packed properly.

As a freight-forwarding agent, I took advantage of this price difference and offered my services collecting, packaging and booking their cargo with airlines. I also took care of the paperwork involved. It was simple logistics, really, but it took a load off my customers' minds and I always looked after their goods as if they were my own.

I picked up business quickly and after three months I was busy enough to employ a secretary. Razna was my first employee and she was excellent. I paid her £4,000 a year and she took care of the paperwork whilst I looked after the customers and their orders. As time went on, I became even busier and started employing couriers to collect goods and professional packers to pack them. One of them, Ray Perkins, is still with me today. In fact, Ray now runs Sea Air & Land Forwarding. He illustrates one of the ways in which I've been able to grow my businesses through collaboration and partnerships with others.

I met Ray when he was working in the courier industry in 1990. I had advertised a position for a manager. After applying, he came in for an interview. I liked him immediately and was impressed by his positive attitude and enthusiasm. I wanted to employ him, but something stopped me. Ray had talked so much during the interview about the courier industry and how lucrative it was. However, he felt he wasn't being appreciated by his employer and I had a better idea that could benefit us both.

I made him a proposal. "How would you like to have your own business?" I said.

"I'd love to," he replied. "But I don't have the money to set up on my own."

"Don't worry," I said. "Let's create a partnership. I'll help you set up a courier business with me as your main client and I'll share my other contacts with you. This way, you can be sure that you will have enough business to get you started. We'll share everything 50/50 – overheads and profits."

To me, this made a lot of sense. I'd be able to work with Ray, take advantage of his abilities and be sure to get the quality of service I wanted from a courier company. He, in turn, would be committed to making the partnership succeed and we would grow together. It would be much better than continuing to use another courier company who had less of an interest in my business.

Ray considered my offer and agreed. He ran his courier company for three years. However, even though he was very good and worked very hard, he found himself up against established businesses in a very competitive industry. It wasn't easy for him to sustain the company in those conditions and over time the company ran up debts of £30,000. Sea Air & Land Forwarding was still growing well and I needed more reliable staff. Ray had impressed me and I wanted to keep him with me. Besides, I felt partly responsible for his situation.

"Look, Ray, we have to dissolve this company because it's not making any profit," I told him. "I'll pay the £30,000 and I'll make you an offer. I want you to run the air freight side of Sea Air & Land Forwarding for me whilst I concentrate on building up the sea freight arm of the business."

Thankfully he said yes. More than 20 years later, Ray now runs all of Sea Air & Land Forwarding and the business is doing well. Even though our courier company didn't succeed I felt sure that partnership was a model that would work. It reflects my general philosophy about life. We cannot succeed in isolation and must work together to make things happen. Over the years, I have created many partnerships with businesses overseas to distribute and sell the products I supply. As the senior partner I am investing in their growth by collaborating with them and giving them every opportunity to succeed. I share their load when necessary and we share each other's success. I never allow my partners to fail. If they fail, I fail. My reputation will be hurt and my business will be damaged. Wherever they are, my partners are almost guaranteed to succeed.

In some ways Sea Air & Land Forwarding was an overnight success and business snowballed. I was picking up customers because I charged a lot less than the department stores' own shipping companies. My overheads were low and I could do the same job for less.

I also went one step beyond my competitors in the same way that I had been taught growing up alongside my brothers in childhood. I found that the way to be successful was to be prepared to do more than the next guy. I took extreme care with the packing and packed everything well. I made sure that people couldn't tell what was inside from looking at the outside so they wouldn't be tempted to steal a TV or a video player or whatever. If something needed a crate, I would put it in a crate and make sure it was properly sealed. I'd deliver it to the cargo shed and make sure everything was shipped safely – and all for less than my competitors. I never cut corners. I've never cut a corner in my life.

However big or small the job, I took the same approach. My attitude was, and still is, that if you are not fit for a small job you are certainly not fit for a bigger one. As far as I was concerned, my reputation travelled on the cargo and it meant everything to me if my customers were happy when receiving the goods. I empathised with them and appreciated how they would feel if the goods that they had shipped with sentimental value had arrived in pieces.

Customers requested all kinds of goods. They would ask:

"Can you pick up some products from Harrods, John Lewis, Selfridges?"

"My child has been studying in the UK and is coming home. Can you pack up his books and ship them?"

"Rami, I bought a bed – can you arrange for it to be shipped abroad?"

I started shipping all kinds of things, from stereos to beds and cutlery to chandeliers. One day I got a call from the Kuwaiti Embassy in London. They'd heard of me by reputation. "The Ambassador of Kuwait is being transferred to Zimbabwe," I was told. "We would like you to pack his belongings for delivery to his new residence in Harare."

"No problem," I said. "I will get a container for you and arrange for his personal belongings to be packed professionally. I will supervise everything myself."

When I said yes, I had no idea just how much we would be transporting. In the end there wasn't just one container but four. It was the biggest job I'd ever done and took weeks to organise and carry out. But I made sure that every single one of the thousands of items were safely and correctly packed. I did it properly; His Excellency had come to me because of my reputation and he was paying me good money not just for a service, but peace of mind. I was very nervous because I knew that this was a chance to consolidate my business. I had to make sure that my service was the best that it could be and that the ambassador had no reason at all to feel concerned about anything. When the containers arrived safely in Zimbabwe with nothing broken or damaged, I breathed a big sigh of relief. His Excellency was delighted and sent me a personal letter to thank me. I still have it today as a reminder of the importance of good service. Every customer deserves it and values it.

My customers recommended me to friends and relatives and the business grew. Their orders became bigger too – hence my decision to build up the sea freight side of the business and take Ray on to look after the air freight. Amongst my customers were people who ran their own businesses, including supermarkets. They were impressed with my services and began asking if I could source and deliver popular British food and drink brands that were unavailable in their own countries. I thought 'Why not?' – after all, it was only logistics, and I had the means to carry out larger-scale deliveries.

It wasn't long before I was collecting large quantities of food and drink from wholesalers and cash and carry's, consolidating them into sea containers and shipping them overseas. My customers were mainly in East and West Africa so you could almost say that I was shipping Marmite to Mali and McVitie's to Mozambique. There were cereals, drinks, biscuits, you name it. British food and drink is popular all over the world because its brands are bywords for quality and taste.

What I didn't realise at first was that in doing this I was saving my customers up to £2,000 per container. This was because, by taking care of every part of the purchasing, consolidation and shipping process, I was cutting out multiple profit centres between the original vendor (such as a wholesaler) to the port of departure. Usually, the overseas buyer would employ a different company for each part of the process, but I took care of the whole thing, saved them money and made a fair profit for myself too. Sourcing products was a brilliant decision that changed the nature of my business and opened the door to the growth that led to our first Queen's Award for Export in 1999 and then to an unprecedented five successive Queen's Awards for Enterprise. However, these rewards were still far away in the late 1980s and early 1990s. Before I could even think about growth on that scale I had to put the foundations in place.

This meant bigger premises, more equipment and more employees. Expansion requires money and you can't always do it with working capital alone. Sometimes you have to get the funds from elsewhere. At the outset this proved to be more difficult that it should have been.

All I ever wanted was an opportunity to prove my worth. Some people gave me that opportunity, but others did not. When I first came to England, few people wanted to employ Asians because we were new arrivals with no track record of success. I had to constantly fight for my talents to be recognised. I had to work harder than the competition just to be given the same chances as them. I had to prove myself again and again. I had to do everything right because I knew people wouldn't give me a second chance.

It's different now. Nowadays, I tell my staff – most of whom are Asian – "You're lucky. Before you, 30–40 years ago, other Asians like me came and we worked hard and proved ourselves. Now you have people ready to employ you, banks willing to lend you money. We are respected."

This wasn't always the case. By 1989, Sea Air & Land Forwarding was growing quickly and I wanted to capitalise on the opportunities this presented. Although I was now in a large double unit at Abbey Self Storage, costing £1,200 a month, it was too small and restrictive – closing at 5.30pm every day and meaning I often had to pack goods at home. If I was to grow my business, and realise the potential that I felt was there, I needed my own premises. As my last shop had shown me, there was little value in leasing. I needed to own my own freehold property.

A freehold warehouse became available in Park Royal, in west London, for £180,000. It was four times the size of the property I was leasing and I'd be able to come and go as I pleased. This would give me independence and enable me to shape my business as I wanted to: I could only do this if I had more warehouse space. I calculated that if I made a deposit of £30,000 from my own money, and got a £150,000 mortgage to buy the warehouse, my monthly repayments would be £1,200 – nearly the same as I was currently paying in rent, but with four times the space. It would be a good move all round but I had to act fast before someone else bought the warehouse.

I made an appointment with my bank manager at NatWest in Hounslow to ask for a loan. I had savings, a house that I was prepared to offer as collateral and a good track record of success. But he just looked at me and said, "It's an over-ambitious plan. I don't think the bank can support it."

I was shocked. I had been with the bank for nearly 15 years, and maintained my personal and business account well. I ran my growing business with a strong balance sheet and the monthly repayments on the loan would be almost the same as I was currently paying in rent for my shed. Furthermore, I was asking for the minimum loan – just 70 per cent. Again I was in tears as I had been when my area manager thwarted me at Dixons. I couldn't believe that people were unwilling to trust me in spite of my track record. I'd set my heart on this warehouse; I'd dreamt and made plans. What could I do now?

I left the bank and crossed the road to another bank. I was frustrated and flustered but I had just one thing in mind – I had to get the money. "I want to see the manager!" I demanded.

"Do you have an appointment?"

"No."

"Do you bank here?"

"No, but I want to see the manager."

I persisted and got to see him. I explained my situation and asked if he would help me. "I'm sorry," he said. "It's not our area."

I was starting to feel desperate. I was very aware that time was running out on an ideal opportunity. Then I saw a branch of Lloyds Bank on the same street. I had nothing to lose, so I decided to try again. I went through the same routine and once again I got to see the manager. This time I got lucky.

"Look," I said, "I am a responsible person and I run my business well. I have savings, a house and will give you my personal guarantee. My business is growing and this loan will enable me to take it to a new level. Now is the right time to do this. I can show you any documents you want to prove that I'm credible."

He didn't ask another question except, "How soon do you want the loan?"

I was amazed. I almost didn't know what to say. "Within seven days," I spluttered. "There's another party interested. We're in a race."

"Don't worry. You'll have it."

He got a motorbike courier to collect the documents he needed to check my credibility and we signed the deal within days. It was amazing.

"Don't worry son, the world runs on the basis of good people," my mother used to tell me. "You just have to find those good people. You will always find somebody somewhere willing to help. God does not come personally to help you," she would say. "He comes through human beings."

After my loan was approved, I thought to myself just how right my mother was.

Later on, I changed banks again. Lloyds moved my account to their Harlesden branch, closer to where I was now operating. The manager there was a nervous type who was always breathing down my neck. It is so important to have a supportive bank manager who trusts you and backs your plans, but this guy was panicky. Whenever a cheque was delayed he'd be chasing me and causing me stress. "Look," I'd say, "you've got my house as security; you've got my personal guarantee. I'm telling you that if sometimes there's a delay, it's OK – bear with me. I have never defaulted or let you down."

Then one day a leaflet came through my door which stated that Barclays was opening a new branch in Park Royal – would I be interested in banking with them? I was unhappy with Lloyds so I went to see them. I've been with Barclays ever since and they've always supported my plans to grow my businesses further. Now, of course, I bank with their corporate team, where they deal in millions of pounds rather than thousands.

However, back in 1989, I just needed £150,000 and I got it. My first warehouse was at 180 Park Avenue, Park Royal and cost £180,000. Two years later, I sold it for £280,000 and bought another for £390,000. I sold that for half a million and bought another again for £1m. In 2000, I bought my current property in Greenford for £4.5m and I've been buying and developing more and more of the property around me as my businesses have grown and more facilities are needed. We now have two units for the shipping company, Sea Air & Land Forwarding, and we've had to buy four warehouses for the marketing company, Sun Mark, because it's grown so big. We converted these four units into one giant warehouse and put in a mezzanine floor where I now have the company's offices. We have also bought two flats and a house locally for staff. We now also have a distribution hub in Dubai and we're developing another one in Miami. It's a huge operation and is getting bigger by the year.

If I'd got that first step wrong, all my subsequent steps would have gone wrong – or never even been possible. However, because I was able to buy a freehold property early on I was able to reduce my costs whilst building up equity. Nowadays my property portfolio must be worth about £25m. It's been a step-by-step process getting to this point and the expansion of premises has been an integral part of the expansion of the businesses. My strong base has enabled me to grow.

9. HEADING FOR THE SUN

'VE ACHIEVED GROWTH not by wild speculation but by building my businesses on solid foundations. I've always tempered risk with caution and avoided making rash decisions. I've never cut corners. I've always done everything in what I believed was the right way. With Sea Air & Land Forwarding I always thought, 'How would I like *my* cargo to be looked after?' and I followed that principle. Most importantly, I've never taken advantage of people or exploited them.

In the early 1990s I was just getting started and was still putting down these foundations. That first warehouse in Park Royal enabled me to take a big step forward. As I said, from dealing with wealthy individuals, I started working with businesses. It was all about logistics – every step had to be timed carefully. If just one delivery from a distributor or wholesaler was late, then the entire shipment would be delayed.

It was just such a delay that opened another door for my business – sourcing directly from manufacturers, rather than via wholesalers and distributors. We had a problem with a distributor for one of my regular customers, Jacky's in Kenya. I had a sea container in my warehouse ready to go to Jacky's, who were running the UN Commissary, with the exception of one thing – a consignment of Cadbury chocolates which were due to be delivered by Cadbury's regular distributor. However, there was no sign of them and we couldn't get hold of the Cadbury's distributor to find out what was going on. My customer, whose entire container was being delayed because of this one delivery, was becoming more and more frustrated. "Can you talk directly to Cadbury?" he asked.

So I did. "Look, your distributor's taken my customer's money and he is not contactable. The warehouse is full with my customer's goods and he needs the chocolates urgently because Christmas is coming. Can I get the products directly from you?"

The lady at Cadbury was sympathetic and asked me: "Do you have an account with us?"

"No," I said.

"OK. Will you pay in advance?"

"Of course."

So I paid the money in advance, collected the goods from Cadbury and got them to my warehouse. Then I told Jacky's the price. "That's 20 per cent cheaper!" they cried. "Can you get us other products as well?"

Of course I said yes and, in doing so, I opened up a Pandora's box. I had no idea of this at the time, as my interest was my shipping business and not in making profit from the sale of goods. I was helping others in order to help myself. I had the infrastructure in place to run a more streamlined procurement, collection, consolidation and delivery operation than most of my competitors because I could do it all myself, rather than outsource any part of the process. I was able to pass the benefit of my 'everything under one roof' approach to my customers by cutting out multiple profit centres between the manufacturers and my customers. In doing so, I was getting my customers' products to them faster, in a fresher state and for less money, and that made me a very attractive prospect. As I often tell my staff, "We make profit whilst buying and if our buying is right, then our selling automatically becomes right."

Now one customer's trust in me had dropped a huge opportunity in my lap and business took off. I owe a great deal to the chairman of Jacky's, the late Ishwar Punjab, for his encouragement and support.

Until 1995, I kept shipping and procurement together under the banner of Sea Air & Land Forwarding. Up to that point, my focus was on shipping and the development of my business had been largely in the hands of my customers. As I explained earlier, when I started Sea Air & Land Forwarding I was getting orders from customers for their electrical goods to be shipped to West Africa, where there was a small manufacturing base. Word-of-mouth recommendation brought me to the attention of electrical wholesalers and they began using me for shipping too. But the market could be precarious – when Japanese companies started building manufacturing and distribution bases in Africa, for example, this market died for me.

This wasn't such a problem, however, because the character of the business changed as my customers led me into new markets. We began to specialise in shipping British food and drink brands to supermarkets overseas. The UK has over 30,000 grocery lines and British brands are highly regarded around the world. This was a reliable platform for growth. Nevertheless, I still didn't feel secure enough because I was very aware that my business development was still very much in the hands of my customers.

The rescue operation with Jacky's and Cadbury had shown me that I needed to become more proactive if I wanted to build a strong, sustainable and growing business. Rather than wait for things to happen – such as another client asking me to oversee a special project for them – I saw that I had to make it happen. Success or failure was in my hands. I already had a well-oiled consolidation and distribution operation, contacts around the world and sales and distribution channels to a growing number of countries. It dawned on me: "Why don't I just ask these big companies if I can become their agent to market their products in countries where they do not have their own distribution channels or agents?"

Operating as a shipping agent for big brands can be a lucrative business. Big British food and drink brands like Fox's, Cadbury, McVitie's, Mars etc. produce a portion of their goods purely for the export market. Because they're selling to wholesalers overseas, they're not incurring any marketing, advertising or distribution costs for the product themselves. As a result, these products can be sold more cheaply than in markets where the brand owners themselves take full responsibility for promoting and marketing the brand. The importer in the destination market picks up the goods at a relatively lower price than their regular commercial value. However, he has to factor his own marketing costs into his business model.

British goods are very popular all over the world, especially food and drink. There are enormous markets for our home manufacturers. But in order for the export model to work, they need shipping agents they can trust. After all, it would be easy for someone from Kenya to buy products at export prices and then re-export the goods back to Britain and cream off the profit that rightfully belongs to, say, Cadbury. There are a lot of good agents out there like us; but there are also a lot of lazy and dishonest ones who might engage in this type of 'parallel trading'. The brand owners need to know they can trust you and be sure that the goods they sell to you will not come back to their own market.

This means that as an agent you need to spend time understanding their markets and building relationships with them as we did. For example, I'm very careful not to compete with their established agents and disturb their existing partnerships. If I know that Cadbury already has a distributor for Singapore, then I won't offer to ship Cadbury products to Singapore. I have access to enough markets and don't need to run a parallel operation. I'm also less expensive than most agents and distributors because I handle the whole process from buying to shipment myself. I take the same care with Cadbury as I would with any of my early individual customers and I try to save them money. This is why we are always in the back of their minds: if an agent or distributor lets them down, they come to us. We have picked up many contracts this way.

The food and drink fraternity is quite small and everyone knows everyone – they meet at industry events, conferences and retail awards. Word spreads. It becomes rather like credit cards: once you have one and your credit is good, people start offering you others. We started with Cadbury. Then Nestlé came on board, then Mars, Unilever and so on. Now we represent almost every major British food and drink brand in specific markets.

We also started shipping a wider range of goods beyond food and drink. In time, we were forwarding toiletries and cleaning products as well – more or less everything you can find in a supermarket. Now we were representing major British food, drink, household and personal care product brands in markets all over the world; we continue to do so to this day.

We've become more than just a freight-forwarder. We build partnerships with potential for growth based on an understanding of the markets that we're selling into. In many cases, for example, we're selling to expat communities who remember the tastes of their childhood or their home country and want to bring that taste into the place where they now live. These are good markets for us. But the success of my business depends on my understanding of what the opportunities are in overseas markets – what sells and what doesn't; where the gaps in the market are; where there is demand but inadequate supply. It was this knowledge that led to the next step – the biggest and most successful move we have made so far: creating our own branded products for export.

By 1995 things were going extremely well. I had larger premises, 30 employees and was pushing Sea Air & Land Forwarding into a new direction, marketing British brands overseas alongside our shipping operation. But the business still wasn't as self-sufficient and secure as I wanted and our destiny was still being shaped by the decisions of others. For example, I found it frustrating that some markets were closed to me for certain products because other agents already had the contract.

I was also very aware how flimsy these contracts could be. From the mid-1990s on, the big companies started to regionalise their distribution centres, particularly in Africa. This had the potential to cause me a lot of pain. For example, over ten years ago I became the number one distributor of Five Alive fruit juices in Nigeria and was turning over £5 million a year from that contract. Then Coca-Cola, who owned Five Alive, built a plant in South Africa to service their African market more quickly, cheaply and profitably. They took the distribution away from me and I lost £5 million of sales a year in one go. This was a huge loss. We had a similar shock with Nestlé, whose chocolate I exported to Kenya.

Nestlé switched to a distribution hub in South Africa and we lost that business too. We were too much at the mercy of other people's moves and I could see the way that the market was going. Relying on others, particularly big brands, always makes for risky business and I was very aware that even though the short-term gains may look great, they could become long-term losses too. We had to adapt or die.

The chance to do so came via another opportune connection made by a satisfied business contact. The general manager of Bestway cash and carry, Mohan Khurana, introduced me to a lady from Nigeria who wanted to buy a particular brand of cooking oil that Bestway itself didn't stock. She asked if I would be able to source and supply it and, of course, I said yes. We managed to source Leisure Cooking Oil from France and started shipping to her business in Nigeria. We also marketed the oil to other customers in Africa and it really took off. Sales were so good, in fact, that in 1995 we created a separate company to market the cooking oil.

We named this new business Sun Oil Limited. I liked the name 'Sun' because it's very auspicious in India; people salute the rising sun. Then I made another decision – one that really opened the floodgates and led directly to where we are today.

I reasoned that our business model was fundamentally fragile: experience had shown me that although we might have the marketing channels for Leisure Oil now, if they changed their distribution network we could be left with nothing, as had happened with Coca-Cola and Nestlé. Our local knowledge also told us that there was a segment of the market that wasn't being catered to by the premium brands we marketed, due to their high cost.

For example, we were big in Nigeria as a distributor but we couldn't sell and distribute McVitie's biscuits there because they already had a distributor. This was fine, but there was a large segment of the biscuit market that could not afford McVitie's. So we decided to approach manufacturers who could produce similar quality products under our own label. We would have products of similar taste and quality to premium brands but at prices that were significantly lower. As a result, we could capture a much bigger slice of the market than just the top end.

Because producing and marketing our own label products would give us greater control over what we sold and where, my destiny would be in my own hands. I felt I had nothing to lose. Venturing into a new area like this might seem a risk, but it wasn't really: food always has value. The worst that could happen would be that we would not make a profit or that we would lose a small amount of money. This was a calculated risk and a case of 'nothing ventured, nothing gained'.

We started with cooking oil. We couldn't call the product Sun Oil because the name was already trademarked, so we called it Laser to depict its sharpness and we sold this successfully into our African markets. This was a good move and we decided to expand our range. Next, we created Pure Heaven, a line of fruit juices. Golden Country followed, our brand for a range of groceries. Then Royalty, our brand for biscuits and selected drinks that we created to celebrate our first Queen's Award in 1999. We've also created brands such as Robust, Bulldog and Bullet, all for energy drinks, Comfi kitchen roll and toilet roll, English Breeze air freshener, Toilet Guard and Sumo bleaches – and so on. We have more than ten of our own brands now, from food and drink to household and personal care products.

As we created more brands and products, our customers started saying to us, "Look, you're selling so many products, like juices etc., but we don't like buying juice from an oil company." They were right, so we changed the name to Sun Mark Ltd, where Mark is short for 'Marketing' – because we were now marketing more than oil alone.

I've always been very ambitious and I've never let any obstacles prevent me from achieving what I've wanted to achieve. I wanted to do something where people took notice. I never wanted to be mediocre, just getting by in life. I actually wanted to create some sensation. Creating Sun Mark was the best business decision I ever made.

10. HOW TO BUILD A BUSINESS THAT GROWS ... AND GROWS

THE LONGEST JOURNEY begins with a single step. We had altered our business model once again and this presented a new challenge to us. We knew how to sell but we didn't necessarily know how to design, brand and promote. However, I followed my instincts and what I had learnt from my many years of selling consumer products to the everyday customer. I understood that the key thing was to use our Britishness as a selling point. Our products are almost solely made in the UK and Britain is famed all over the world for the quality and taste of its food and drink.

A brand begins with the name. The names we choose for our brands are very important because they have to instantly create the right image and association in the mind of a customer. An inappropriate name can hinder progress.

For example, the brand name Heinz to me does not communicate the profile of the product. It's a family name and not a good name for foodstuffs. But because Heinz is more than 150 years old, it has built its reputation over a very long time with massive advertising over the years and everyone now knows that Heinz makes food. I can't do that – I can't call my brands Ranger, because I don't have the time or the money to educate consumers about my brand through television and radio advertising, poster campaigns and so on. I'm not the first in the market like Heinz was, so I have to create an immediate association which means something to people straightaway.

The name 'Golden Country', for example, suggests the countryside and fields where crops are grown. It represents nature's freshness and goodness. Royalty came about after Sea Air & Land Forwarding won its Queen's Award in 1999, as mentioned previously. We said, "Royalty has been graciously pleased to give us this award, so let's celebrate this". And the Royalty brand has been very successful: people immediately think of the tradition, quality and Britishness that the UK's royalty represents. English Breeze implies the freshness of the English countryside. Toilet Guard – although it is nothing special – says straightaway what it does, unlike Toilet Duck. But, you see, the makers of Toilet Duck have the money to market and promote the brand widely. I don't. I have to make brands that cause people to think "Oh, I know this." I need them to almost have a sense of déjà vu. Even with the company name, Sun Mark: Sun represents light and life; Mark tells you that we are a marketing company and market brands, and also that we are making our mark in the world. It works.

A good brand name can also give people a feel-good factor. For example, Tesco's and Sainsbury's value label products use the same branding for every product from toilet roll to butter. The packaging is very plain because their aim is to emphasise to people that they are buying a value-range product. This is all very well, but in my experience customers are discerning and don't need to be told so blatantly that they are buying good value products. They don't want to be reminded that they are on a budget – they want to feel that they are making a clever purchase by getting a quality product at a good price. 'Value range' branding feels cheap to me. If these products were marketed under exciting names, then the same products would give customers a much better feeling about their purchases. Personally, I feel that customers should not have to buy the same brand of toilet roll and butter. There are different kinds of products for different uses and purposes.

But a brand's name alone is not enough, though important. There's a good deal more to achieve before you can build a successful business. You need the right quality of products at the right price; you need distribution channels so that products reach the customer; and you need to persuade the customer to set aside their loyalty to other brands and try yours. I've actually built Sun Mark on a relatively simple formula, but our growth has been dependent on getting every step right so that we have an efficient and effective operation on a strong base. I knew from the start that we would have to plan carefully, be patient and do the right things. I was confident that if the product was good and the price was good, people would like it. If I could then make it easily available and accessible, I would build trust and confidence and people would buy it.

Then I believed – correctly – that it would really take off if we followed the right growth strategy. There are three fundamental ways to grow a business: through mergers, acquisitions or strategic alliances. I've never been interested in merging with another business or buying something that has already been created by someone else. It's too complicated and means you have to undo someone else's vision before you can implement your own. I would far rather do things my way from the start.

So we've built Sun Mark through adopting the third growth strategy – strategic alliances. From the start I have followed a calculated strategy of building beneficial partnerships into our manufacturing and distribution processes. The first alliance we made was with the manufacturers and was based on the understanding that there are parallel markets for every food and drink product you can think of – a premium market and a budget market.

Creating branded products for the premium market is costly because brands need a huge amount of promotion. The cost of advertising, marketing, a sales force etc. can be huge. These all add a percentage to the price paid by the consumer. For example, McVitie's Digestives become a premium product, even though they may actually be relatively cheap to make in high volumes. The price is within the reach of expats and affluent consumers in the markets we sell into, but beyond the reach of the majority of people. Think about Chanel perfume – you are paying for the bottle, the model, the adverts, and these costs may be more than the actual cost of producing the perfume inside the bottle.

A digestive biscuit is a digestive biscuit. Baked beans are baked beans. Cornflakes are cornflakes. But when people walk into a supermarket, they pick out the brand they trust. They grab what they know and they're gone. Brands are trust and they become power as a result, and this is why companies spend so much time and money building their image, profile and reputation. A Chanel bag will be bought by people who want to make a statement. They're not going to buy a cheaper bag even if it's of the same style and quality. They're going to buy Chanel. People who want premium brands are going to buy Mercedes, Fox's, Heinz, because they want to feel 'I am buying the best'.

But at the same time, there's another market where people can't afford to buy a Chanel bag but they still need a bag. They can't afford a Mercedes but they still need a car. They can't afford Fox's but they still want a biscuit as a treat.

There's room in every marketplace for both because there are parallel markets for products at different price points that fulfil people's same basic needs. So why should we not have two bites of the cherry by offering both branded and secondary brand products to customers? We approached manufacturers of brands whose products we already distributed and asked, "Please pack your products under our own label and we'll sell them into markets you have not tapped. We don't have the same marketing and branding costs as yours, so we'll be able to sell at a lower shelf price into the middle income group."

This was a smart move, because even though we were selling a similar product, produced by the same manufacturer, we were not actually competing with them. We were not taking their business away. In fact, we were creating a bigger market for their products by servicing both ends of the market, thus increasing their overall volume of business. This was a win-win situation; neither of us could lose. We now had two possibilities in every market – an established premium brand which we distributed on someone else's behalf and our own brand, which we marketed and sold as we pleased to the middle market.

The former gives us prestige and good entry points into new markets; the latter gives us security through an entirely independent source of revenue.

Our customers can't lose either, because it's with our customers that we build our second set of strategic alliances. We find customers at trade exhibitions all over the world and we invest in the material to make an impact there as we exhibit our products. After all, hidden talent is no talent. If you have good products and services, then you must broadcast that to the world, let people know what you can offer them and what benefit you can bring. In the first two-thirds of 2013 alone, we've exhibited in China, Dubai, New York, Washington, Barcelona, Madrid, Trinidad and Azerbaijan. I've personally been to St Petersburg, Istanbul and Germany. Wherever there are serious food exhibitions we are present, because that's where we find genuine customers.

We look for people with vision and knowledge. We want to sell to people with ambition for their business but who are adaptable and able to complement what we do. We want customers who understand what we require and who will work cooperatively to our mutual benefit. It's not enough for me just to sell to them and leave them alone; I support them with a business strategy, marketing and sometimes with resources. My aim is to help them grow their business because their success is my success and I cannot afford to let them down. As I say to them, "I can afford to lose money, but I can't afford to lose a customer". Money I can earn back; but once I lose a customer because of poor service or products, he will take another ten with him. Negative publicity travels faster than lightning. We are interdependent. As a businessman, I am not like a hunter going in for a quick kill; I am more like a farmer working over the year for a bumper crop.

Although I am cooperative and supportive in the way I conduct my partnerships, I am not naïve and I am certainly not a pushover. Although I was lazy in my childhood and spent too much time hanging around with the wrong crowd, I got to know more about people's characters than I would have done if I had simply been studious. I learnt to recognise people's real motives and not to take them at face value but to check them out first. I became streetwise – I had to be and I still am. I analyse people and reason with myself and see if what they say is plausible. If they are a business, I do due diligence and check their trading record to make sure that what they say stands up. I always take the view that if something sounds too good to be true, then it isn't true.

I also maintain a strict credit policy based on an Indian proverb: *"Secure your house and don't call anyone a thief"*. To start with, I don't give credit to overseas clients because the complexities of international banking make this difficult to monitor and manage. So I ask for either payment in advance or a letter of credit and I explain to my customers that any delays in payment from them will mean that I have to delay my payment to my suppliers which will delay their shipment. It will also mean that I have to employ more people to manage debts, and then I will have to increase my prices. So it's in their interests to pay me promptly. This results in me controlling my overheads and keeping my prices competitive. Besides, I do not wish to act as a banker or suffer bad debts that can destroy my business.

For companies based in the UK, I insist on a director's personal guarantee. In the event of a company going into receivership, I look to the director for payment. I follow the principle of banks in this regard. People who want my goods must be able to guarantee payment personally; if someone does not have faith in themselves and their business, then why should I put my faith in them? With blue-chip companies, of course, we offer credit – we know that they have a strong and established balance sheet and are not going to default on their payment in a hurry.

Managing a business like Sun Mark is all about paying attention to details in order to keep everything in balance. If one thing goes out of balance – such as a delayed payment from a customer – then everything goes out of balance. To avoid this, we have safeguards in place, from the vetting of customers through to the management of payment. Throughout, we conduct ourselves honestly and honourably and we expect our partners to do the same. That's what partnership is: we share the costs and the work and, finally, the profit. It's well worth it, because in doing so we double or even quadruple our strength and that enables Sun Mark to compete successfully against much bigger players in a fiercely competitive marketplace.

This is the machinery that supports the brands we create. But it would count for nothing if we didn't have good quality products that people want. The final step in the process is marketing to consumers themselves. The success of my business depends on my understanding of what consumers want and what the opportunities are in overseas markets. We rely heavily on local knowledge, which we build up at the exhibitions we attend and by talking to our customers in order to help us expand and find new markets. For example, we recently shipped a container to Mongolia. Mongolia has an annual growth rate of 17 per cent. It's growing faster than China. How many people know that? We find a local partner, we expand our regional network to include them, and the job is almost done. One cannot overestimate the value a local commander can bring to the business.

I mentioned that the power of brands lies with the loyalty that they generate. When shopping, people go straight to the brands they know, fill their basket, pay and leave. They don't even have the time to see if there is another product that offers better quality and price. They just pick up the brands they trust. Getting people to switch brands and trust your product is a challenge.

Over the years, I have learnt that there are effective marketing strategies. Firstly, you can spend a great deal of money on TV, radio or press advertising to create brand awareness. This is very effective but will undoubtedly increase the cost of the products and is one of the main reasons why premium brands cost as much as they do. We aim to pitch to consumers at a different price point from the premium brands and we keep commercial advertising to a minimum. Nevertheless, we do advertise in some markets where we have strong sales and want to reinforce our brand profile and increase the strength of our presence by helping our customers grow. Pure Heaven juices are very popular in the Caribbean and Africa, for example, and it makes sense to capitalise on that popularity with television advertising. We pay for the advertising, our local distributors generate more sales and their business grows. As their business grows, they buy more from us and we grow too. It's in my interest to support my customers in this way. I say to them, "Anyone will give you directions to New York but they will not give you the fare. I will give you both and you won't lose any money because I will cover your losses if they ever occur."

The second strategy is time. If a brand is strong enough to remain in the market for long enough, its profile will simply grow organically. People will buy it because they are familiar with it and consumers trust products they are familiar with. It's the ones they don't recognise that they don't trust quickly.

This is why the third strategy, sampling, is by far the most cost-effective way to market a product. If you give people a free sample to try, they have nothing to lose. If they like it you build trust instantly. You allow the product to do the talking and in doing so you limit your marketing spend and keep the cost to the consumer down. If customers are satisfied with the taste and quality and if they recognise that the product represents good value for money, they will switch loyalty and buy your brand.

Giving away free samples has been the most powerful marketing tool for Sun Mark. We give samples away at exhibitions to potential customers to persuade them to buy from us. Once they become our customers, we give them more free samples to give to their customers. Finally, everything comes down to the quality of the product you sell; quality has an immediate impact and speaks for itself.

I have built Sun Mark on the basis of quality in every area of operation. We are about quality in our relationships, in our business processes, in our service and in our products. From the bottom of the business to the top, I pay attention to detail and ensure everything is as good as it can be. As they say, excellence endures long after everything else is forgotten. I have made bold decisions but each step I've taken has been planned carefully and thought through properly. We weren't greedy, and made sure we kept within our resources and built one step at a time. It has paid off handsomely and I've been able to keep all sides of my businesses going – freight-forwarding, acting as an agent for big brands and now creating and selling my own brands. I have created a very powerful business model that has been a fantastic platform for growth; in fact, the quality of the processes I have created is so good that the business almost grows by itself now.

As I write, we export to 110 countries, the turnover is touching £180 million and growing, and so is the profit – which is around £15 million. In 2009, Sun Mark received its first Queen's Award for Enterprise in international trade. To be given a Queen's Award you have to meet very tough criteria. You have to show more than 30 per cent growth for three years in a row; you have to generate employment; you have to be an ethically and environmentally friendly business; you have to demonstrate innovation; and you have to show how you are bringing tangible benefits to the British economy. It's very hard to earn one and they are given only to the most successful businesses.

In 2010 we won another Queen's Award for Enterprise in international trade. Then again in 2011, 2012 and 2013. No other company has even won three in a row before, but we have won five. It's unprecedented. It's a record achievement and one that I'm extremely proud of. What's more, it has been achieved during a recession in the UK, with a global downturn in trade. But we have been smart – we have expanded in oil-rich and developing countries. We have targeted parts of the world like Mongolia that are experiencing economic growth.

Sun Mark has also received other awards and accolades. For the last three years, it has featured in the *Sunday Times* Profit Track 100 and we have made our way into the top quarter of the most successful British businesses. We have been made a National Champion by the European Business Awards. In 2013, I was personally made the Institute of Directors' "Director of the Year" for Large Business in London and the South East. I am increasingly in demand as a spokesman on British business issues for the media. In January 2013 I was even invited to debate multiculturalism at the Cambridge Union Society. All of these accolades tell me that I have succeeded and that all of my efforts for so many years have been worthwhile.

Sun Mark is continuing to grow. I expect turnover to hit £180 million next year, then a quarter of a billion, then half a billion and so on. Our products are in so many places that if one market suffers I can direct resources elsewhere; I am protected by the breadth of my operation. I have built a business that is growing and growing and growing and I see no sign or reason for it to slow down as long as people continue to eat.

In a way, this is more than I ever dreamed of. Coming from a very poor family, I only wanted security for tomorrow for myself and my family. Indian people often have this same wish, as they have been accustomed to India where there is no safety net or social security. We can only rely on ourselves or our children to look after us when we are older: nobody else will. That's why we're so good to our children. They say that when you lose, you don't lose a lesson. I learned my lesson from what happened with Coca-Cola and Nestlé and built a more solid foundation for my business. Besides, I feel that you must test your mettle. Even though I am cautious in the risks I take, I take them because if you don't listen to your instincts and follow your dreams, you have already lost in life. The worst that can happen is that you will end up where you started – in my case, with nothing. But who knows? You may move a lot faster and further. After all, if you do nothing you achieve nothing. If you do something, you may surprise yourself. You might just achieve everything.

Presenting the Queen's Award cufflinks to
the Mayor of London, Boris Johnson, in
April 2012.

With my friend the Rt Hon Dominic Grieve
QC MP, in November 2012. Dominic is now the
Attorney General for England and Wales. I have
known him since 2006.

Renu and I met the Foreign Secretary, the Rt Hon David Miliband MP, in 2009. Although a member of the Conservative Party, I consider it important to mix with politicians across the spectrum.

With Indian icons Mr S. P. Hinduja and G. P. Hinduja at our third Queen's Award party at the Grosvenor Hotel, Park Lane, London in October 2011.

I met Margaret Thatcher on several occasions; this picture was taken at the residence of Hon Bernard Jenkin MP in 2011. Like many, I consider Baroness Thatcher one of Britain's greatest prime ministers – without her economic legacy, building Sun Mark would have been a far harder task.

With the current prime minister at 10 Downing Street in October 2011. Mr Cameron continues to be extremely supportive of the work we do to promote Britain overseas and to foster good relations between Britain's diverse communities.

With Shri Salman Khurshid, Cabinet Minister for India's Ministry of External Affairs, in June 2013 at the Oxford-India Day. A lawyer and writer as well as a politician, Mr Khurshid has done a great deal to defend the rights of minority groups in India.

Renu and I with the Rt Hon David Cameron MP in December 2009 when he was campaigning in Finchley. Mr Cameron has done a great deal to modernise the Conservative Party and to bring Asians into the Tory fold. We're his big supporters.

I proudly received my MBE in 2005 from HRH the Prince of Wales for services to British Business and the Asian Community. His Royal Highness is a great supporter of young people in Britain and I am proud to be a fellow of the Prince's Trust, helping underprivileged young people join the next generation of entrepreneurs like me.

Shaking hands with Her Majesty the Queen at Buckingham Palace during a reception hosted for Queen's Award winners, 2010. I'm very proud to have received honours from Her Majesty the Queen on seven occasions.

(Left) I was presented with my very first Queen's Award – for export – in 1999. It took a while to earn the second, but now we can't stop winning!

(Above) Being presented with the Queen's Award for Enterprise in 2011 by the Lord-Lieutenant of Greater London, Sir David Brewer CMG, JP. At the time this was Sun Mark's third successive Queen's Award – a record. Now we have won five.

(Right) Receiving the NRI Businessman of the Year Award by the NRI Institute from Mr Shashi Tharoor, Indian Minister for External Affairs, in India 2010 at Le Meridian Hotel, New Delhi.

(Left) I am now fortunate enough to own a Rolls-Royce Ghost, pictured here in 2011, when once I could not afford a bicycle.

(Right) Receiving the prestigious Growing Business Awards, Export Champion of the Year 2013, and *(below)* with the other winners.

11. THE IMPORTANCE OF VISION AND LEADERSHIP

WHEN I STARTED out on my own in a self-storage shed in Hayes, I simply wanted to build a respectable company that would provide me with a good living. I had no idea that within three decades I would be at the head of an operation with an annual turnover of more than £180 million and growing. Nor did I dream that one of my companies would win an unprecedented five consecutive Queen's Awards or that I would be awarded an MBE. What I have achieved with Sun Mark shows that with vision, ambition and determination anything is possible in Britain – you can achieve whatever you want to achieve.

As Sun Mark grew, my vision changed. From simply wanting a respectable business, I now want to build a world-class company and leave a good legacy behind me for my family and community. The platform that I built at the very outset has made this bigger, more ambitious vision possible. Driven by my expanding ambition the vision has grown with every successful step. It's the logic of life: a man wants a suit and once he gets a suit, he wants another. When he feels he has enough suits, he wants a car; then he wants a bigger car, then a house, then a bigger house – and so on. His ambition grows with each new accomplishment.

So my vision has expanded step by step. None of the growth I have experienced has happened by accident. It has been a series of measured steps, with each move thought through carefully and implemented with the support of the people I have around me. Running a business like this is not a one-man show and I would not have got where I am today without others who have understood and helped me to realise my vision. My wife, Renu, has been a rock for me as I have said before. In addition, there are also my employees – from Ray Perkins onwards. They have been an integral part of the formula that has created the success we are now experiencing. I now employ 120 people. We have transport drivers, warehouse people, forklift truck drivers, cleaners, order processors, accountants, trademark lawyers, salespeople and graphic designers. Sun Mark is a big operation and everybody plays their part to keep it running smoothly in order to help it grow.

It's important that they all understand the vision and values that lie behind it. I lead from the front, set the example and show my employees in my own behaviour what I expect from them. Recruiting people who share the company values and developing them in the right way is essential to any business and I pay particular attention to these aspects of Sun Mark. At the initial stage of recruitment we have a simple checklist of qualities that we're looking for: firstly, we want people who are within short commuting distance of the office or who are willing to relocate; we look for people who are stable and haven't chopped and changed their jobs three to four times in a year; we look for good English language skills, mathematical skills and computer literacy; and of course, we look for relevant experience for the role. But above all, I am looking for adaptability and ambition in a candidate. My staff conduct interviews, create a shortlist and then I come in for the final interview and selection to make sure the person will fit into the Sun Mark jigsaw.

At this point, I am looking at them as raw material. It doesn't matter to me if they have a few rough edges because I am interested in their potential. When it comes to developing people under my leadership, I think of myself as a tailor. I can make a good shirt if the material is good. So it is essential from the very outset to recruit people who are the right material. Nobody is born a doctor, an engineer or a businessman – they have to be coached, guided and tailored. The most important quality I look for in a new staff member is the desire to progress in life. This means I want people with ambition, flexibility, a positive attitude and the ability to get on with people.

To me, a person's attitude is the key to their success. I always say that in Britain, if you are poor it's because you have a poor attitude. Britain is not a poor country and there is no reason to be poor here unless you have a health issue of some kind. If people like me can come from developing countries and become successful despite all the handicaps, drawbacks and prejudices we have had to overcome, then there is no reason why someone born and raised in Britain cannot become successful. I would love to find the magic bullet that enables one to become successful without having to work for it, but there isn't one. There is no substitute for hard work.

Yet so many people need outside motivation to work; they almost need to be pushed to do it. Generally, I find that people in the workplace work for three reasons: the first is money, and people motivated by this stop working the moment they feel they've earned their pay. The second is fear, and people motivated by this only work hard if they are afraid of being sacked or criticised. The best employees work for their own self-respect and ambition. They are self-motivated and want to get somewhere in life so nobody has to push them, tell them to work or instruct them on exactly what they have to do. They are keen to make their mark.

As the saying goes, God helps those who help themselves. So, when recruiting, I look for people with the qualities I have described. I believe ambitious people benefit their family, their community and their country. Ambitious, but not ruthless: I would never try to achieve my aims by treading on other people and I don't like to see this in other people either. Ambition must be tempered with empathy, loyalty and an understanding that business is not a race but a lifelong endeavour. It takes time and patience to build success on solid foundations and success like this is lasting and genuinely rewarding.

So I look for ambition and loyalty. Loyalty, to me, is the prerequisite for success and I doubt whether I would have been as successful had I not been loyal to my adopted country, Britain. In my employees, loyalty is more important to me than whether someone is super-bright or highly educated. I want people who will remain, grow with me and help me develop my business. I am allergic to high-flyers, the kind of people who are always looking for the next big thing and who jump from job to job because they believe there is a shortcut to success when there isn't. They consume money, resources and feel they should be rewarded all the time just because of who they are. People like this would do more harm than good to Sun Mark. Besides, if they were as clever as they think they are, they wouldn't be working for someone else – they would be running their own business.

When I worked at Dixons and managed their Cheapside store, I had no choice about who I employed. The company would send new people in and I would have to work with them within the parameters set by Dixons. We all knew these parameters and so it worked. But when I started my own company and began employing people for myself, I had to learn a much wider range of management skills to ensure that my staff were able to perform to the best of their abilities within the parameters I set at Sun Mark. To a large extent, I am guided by a simple proverb: *"If I treat you the way you are, then I will be instrumental in keeping you as you are. But if I treat you as you ought to be, then I will be instrumental in making you as you ought to be."* I believe this firmly. So I set expectations and I explain them clearly. I care for my staff but I don't let them get away with anything. I am firm but fair and if I ever have reason to rebuke someone, I will always explain the logic and the rationale behind the rebuke. I find that they respect me more for taking the trouble to do this than if I had just criticised them and moved away.

I reward people who need to be rewarded and I promote from within wherever possible. But I always tell my employees that they should not expect too much too soon and they should be prepared to work their way up from the bottom to the top. Even if their job is just cleaning cars, as mine once was, they must make sure the car is gleaming and their employer or customer can see that it's been cleaned with effort. Mediocrity gets you nowhere, but excellence is noticed. I tell people that efforts are in their hand and rewards are in the hands of God. In fact, rewards are also in our own hands.

As a leader, I will never tell my staff to do a job that I wouldn't be prepared to do myself. Moreover, a leader also has to be smarter than the people around him. Nobody who is better than you will work for you. They'll simply think, "Why am I working for this fool? He's a total waste of time." When my staff are smart, I have to be smarter. This means I have to be ahead of the game. I have no divine right to be respected, followed or listened to. I have to think deeply, plan carefully and always stay a step ahead of the people around me. Running a business and being a leader of others is a constant self-motivating exercise. I can't flag for a moment. Every day I have to demonstrate to the people around me what it takes to be successful.

As the business has grown, I have had to learn a range of managerial skills that I didn't need before. I have had to learn how to delegate and follow up and I expect my managers to do the same. I always say to them: "Before you settle down and get on with your work for the day, make sure your staff are busy." It's a simple thing but it's easy to overlook and it ensures that everyone is productive and doing what they should be doing. If someone is underperforming or causing problems, I am willing to work with them rather than get rid of them. I am patient and believe that people can be turned around with the right guidance. Why would I sack someone who I have employed, paid and trained?

Recruitment is expensive and I want to keep it to a minimum. I believe in finding a cure rather than surgery. We're not machines and sometimes we just need someone to show empathy and guide us along the right path. For me, the cure is simple logic: if you do good, you will receive good. This is logical to me. So I explain to my staff the logic of being positive, of being productive, of adding value to what they do for the company and for themselves – the logic of self-respect that earns the respect of others. This is the cure to me. Surgery, sacking someone – that is a last resort.

The fact that our staff turnover is so low and that many of my staff have stayed with me for so long tells me that my approach to recruitment and development is the right one for Sun Mark. You see, business is all about people: money doesn't make money; people make money. If you want to build a business that is sustainable and grows, then your people need to feel motivated, rewarded and happy to be doing what they do. You need to be clear about what you expect from them, quick to correct errors or wrong turns and lead by setting an example in everything you do. My vision encompasses all of the relationships that drive Sun Mark – with suppliers, customers and employees. If one is out of synch, all are out of synch. So I make sure we share the investment, effort and the reward. We share the vision that has turned Sun Mark into one of the most successful companies in the world.

I choose the people I work with carefully, whether they are employees, suppliers or customers and I go with people who understand that we are united in working towards a common goal: success. With customers, for example, I take time to establish the nature of their business, their market and what they actually need. I don't just sell to them but bring my knowledge and wisdom to bear on what they do and how they do it. For example, if they can sell ten boxes of Pure Heaven, I will only sell them ten boxes. But if I see that they'll struggle to sell ten boxes, then I won't sell them that many because it will just put a block on their capital, their warehouse space and the goods could even expire. "These aren't collector's items," I'll tell them. "You can always come back and buy more."

I'll often use the analogy of the two medical students who go to the same college, study the same subject from the same books with the help of the same professors in the same building. Yet one ends up as a respected Harley Street physician, the other a seedy backstreet surgeon performing dodgy operations. Why? Because the one in Harley Street listens to his patients and takes the time to diagnose their ailments correctly; he spends time finding the right treatment and will seek a second opinion, if necessary. The other is simply in a hurry to see the next patient, to make a quick buck and move on. It takes time and patience to build a strong business and I won't allow my customers to overstock or buy the wrong products because they are impatient for success. I get them to understand that we are in a mutually beneficial relationship and that their success is my success and vice-versa.

I try to be an asset in everything I do. I try to add value to people's businesses and their lives. It's a matter of respect for me – earning the respect of others and maintaining one's self-respect is essential at all times. I cannot allow myself to cause anyone any loss. If I do, then my reputation suffers along with my business. I suffer too, personally; I feel that I have made a mistake, become a liability. Perhaps this is what drives me. If so, it is what drives my businesses too. My vision is to be an asset to everyone – my family, my friends, my customers, my suppliers, my employees and to Great Britain itself – a country that has rewarded me greatly since my arrival. I am very much my father's son.

12. IN MY FATHER'S FOOTSTEPS

ALTHOUGH I NEVER met my father, his life has influenced mine profoundly. He was always present during my childhood in my mother's memories of him and in the values he passed on to my brothers and sister. With me, it was through the documents my mother rescued from our home before our evacuation, and his reputation. His reputation also gave us opportunities we might otherwise not have had. I couldn't help but grow up aware that I was the son of a great man who died and was hailed a martyr for a just cause.

I turned away from his values as a teenager when I was lazy and thought the world owed me a living. As an adult, I rediscovered his principles and I have spent my life since trying to live up to them and to be everything my father would have wanted me to be. Above all, I have tried to be the person that I myself would respect. No one has a divine right to be respected – it's up to us to earn it by showing the world that we can benefit others through our lives.

The desire to earn the respect of others can drive you to achieve great things. In 2005, I was awarded the MBE by Her Majesty the Queen. I got it because I worked hard to build a successful business and also devoted my time to benefit my community through various social, charitable and political activities. My citation read *"For services to British business and the British Asian community"*.

I was extremely proud of achieving such an honour as an Indian immigrant to the UK. When I first arrived in 1971, the Indian community was struggling and was not taken seriously. What the British people knew of India was what they saw on television – images of poverty, overcrowded trains and wars with Pakistan. It took us a long time to earn the respect of the locals and show them that we were honest, intelligent, hardworking people and an asset. For example, I had a friend who on arriving in Britain applied for a job as a postman. While he was waiting for his interview, there were other postmen standing around and he heard them saying to each other, "Can we trust him with our post?"

He had to bite his tongue. 'I was a headteacher in India,' he thought to himself. 'I had a great deal of respect there and here you are asking each other if you can trust me with your post?'

There was a terrible ignorance about India and Indians when we first started to arrive in the UK in numbers and we experienced a great deal of prejudice. On one occasion, a Sikh friend of mine who wore a turban took his family to Brighton for a break and wanted to stay the night in a bed and breakfast that clearly had a sign saying 'Vacancies'. But he was told there were no vacancies and he had to return back to London with his family in humiliation. This kind of prejudice was normal when I arrived in Britain and I experienced it myself during the years I worked for others. My attitude towards prejudice was simple: "I must ignore it and just get on with what I'm doing. I'll let my work do my talking for me." There's a saying that when people don't like you, it's because they don't know you; but they don't know you because they don't like you. My fellow Indians and I had to break this cycle by being positive and working hard to achieve results so that people would recognise, appreciate and respect our good qualities.

With time and a positive attitude one can overcome preconceived perceptions and prejudices as we have. We early arrivals from India have paved the way for the second, third and even fourth generations of British Indians to grow up, be educated and work alongside everyone else with minimal prejudice. At one time, the British couldn't stand Indian curry and now they can't get enough of it. It has become a national dish. We Indians, too, have now become an integral part of British society.

This has also been the Indian experience everywhere. The diaspora since independence means there are now more than 25 million Indians living around the world. Practically 50 per cent of the populations of Guyana, Trinidad and Fiji are Indian. We didn't just go to the West, but to South Africa, East Africa, West Africa and the Caribbean to name but a few places. In fact, wherever the Brits went, they took us with them to help them with their Empire. I have cousins in Canada, the USA and Australia. Wherever we go, we integrate well because we are the product of a secular and democratic nation and we have been taught to use merit and not race or religion to surge ahead. The fact that so many races, cultures and religions can live side by side in India demonstrates the Indian ethos of peaceful coexistence.

We are also entrepreneurial people and our spread around the world has been driven by trade and business. With more than a billion people living in India, the competition for jobs is intense. So wherever we see an opportunity, we go. It used to be mainly people from Gujarat and Punjab. Gujaratis were traders by tradition and Punjabis were in the British Armed Forces and were also uprooted due to the division of Punjab at the time of the partition of India in 1947. But now even the South Indians, the 'true' Indians, are spreading out. Being very good at maths, they are travelling to the USA in big numbers to become software programmers to support the tech boom.

Being part of an immigrant population is a balancing act. On the one hand, you want to integrate comfortably into your new society, and on the other you want to preserve the culture and traditions that give you your identity and strength. Indians support each other very well wherever they go and I have been involved with many organisations since arriving in Britain. It's almost like a hobby for me, but one that helps to spread social harmony. Some people play golf or go fishing but I like meeting people and being involved with them. Plus, it's a great honour when somebody appoints you as president of an organisation and an award is an award, no matter how big or small. As I write, I am chairman of the British Sikh Association, the Pakistan India and UK Friendship Forum, president of the Punjabi Society of the British Isles and chairman of the Golden Heart Club, as well as a patron of many other organisations and fellow of the Prince's Trust.

All of the organisations I am involved with do significant work for the community and many aim to combat prejudice and bring people from different cultures together. I'm led by my father and Mahatma Gandhi, whose outlooks were very similar: both men fought against the partition of India and opposed theocracy, arguing that unity across religious and cultural divides would make India stronger. As an adult it has become almost natural for me to advocate Gandhi's principles of justice, unity, independence and advancement by merit. Gandhi was also a pragmatist as am I, and I believe that whatever our differences in politics, culture or religion there is usually a mutual benefit in collaboration and partnership. We are stronger when we work together and populations develop more wholesomely in democratic and secular societies. Religion is important because it offers peace of mind; but I can't use religion to pay my electricity bill or buy a new car. I have to work for that and earn it through my own merit. Besides, I believe that God only helps those who help themselves.

The British Sikh Association promotes interfaith dialogue and peaceful coexistence between Sikhs and the wider diverse British community in line with the teachings of the Sikh Gurus. We believe the role of religion should be to unite mankind not to drive a wedge between people as so often seems to be the case. Everybody has the right to live and to coexist with others no matter what food they eat, clothes they wear or religion they practise.

I'm also president of the Punjabi Society of the British Isles, which is the oldest Indian society in Britain. It was founded in 1928 to preserve Punjabi culture and heritage at a time when there was just a handful of Punjabis in Britain. We Punjabis have made Britain a richer place. Punjabi food has driven the growth in popularity of Indian restaurants in the UK and our dress has influenced British fashion. Punjabi Bhangra music has found its way into British mainstream music. Even our language has influenced the way that teenagers of all cultures speak in modern Britain.

Ours is not the only culture to enrich Britain, of course. London, in particular, is a very cosmopolitan city where Asians, Greeks, Turks, Chinese, West Indians, Africans and Europeans live side by side beneath the Union flag. Its diversity is one of the reasons London was awarded the Olympic Games and we all contributed to that in one way or another. My father used to say, "India's diversity and unity are like the colours of a rainbow and its charm will diminish if one were removed."

My work with the Hindu Forum of Britain illustrates this point further. Though not a Hindu myself, I am a founder member of the forum, which was set up to unite all the different Hindu organisations in Britain under one umbrella so that they could project a cohesive voice to British government departments. I campaigned vigorously against the frivolous depiction of Hindu deities in derogatory ways such as on carrier bags, shoes and other items of clothing which I felt were defamatory towards Hindus. I organised the first Hindu Ball at the Hilton Hotel in Park Lane, London, to celebrate Hindu culture and its contribution to British society.

When I see disharmony, intolerance, disrespect and prejudice, I want to overcome it. It's almost an obligation to me. Like my father, I fight my cause passionately and persistently. One of the most important things I have done is promote dialogue and friendship between Indians and Pakistanis living in the UK. The trouble here is that even though we are thousands of miles away from our motherlands, when Pakistan and India catch a cold their expat communities in Britain sneeze. And, with close to two million Indians and a million Pakistanis – not to mention Bangladeshis – living in Britain today, this is a serious problem for social harmony. It wasn't until a wave of suicide bombings by Islamist extremists that killed 52 people on London streets on 7 and 21 July 2005 that I realised just how damaging our rivalry could become.

The political philosopher Edmund Burke said, *"The only thing necessary for the triumph of evil is for good men to do nothing."* Like most Indians, I had grown up distrustful of Pakistanis, and my father's prediction proved correct that the creation of a theocracy would plunge India and Pakistan into decades of conflict. I thought about this and the fact that continuing to be rivals within an entirely different country and culture was completely pointless. In fact, Indians and Pakistanis have common history, heritage and culture. There is far more that unites us than divides us. I felt I had to do something. We needed to draw a line under the past and say, "Look, we've got our countries now and they weren't made to become rivals. We need to learn to respect each other and live together."

My father had died not hating Muslims who wanted their own country. In fact, he was pleading for all of India's communities to live together. I said to myself, "Let me see if I can promote his ethos and unite Indians and Pakistanis in the UK." I thought if I could unite even ten people I would have achieved a great deal.

As it happens, I have been able to help bring Indians and Pakistanis living in Britain together on a much larger scale. A year after the bombings, in 2006, I met Arif Choudhary, who had travelled to London from Pakistan to set up a British arm of the Pakistan India Friendship Society that he had founded. Arif and I found we had a common outlook and he invited me to become the chairman of the new Pakistan India and UK Friendship Forum. We launched the forum on 8 February 2007 at the House of Commons, with many prominent figures from both communities in attendance. Later that year, on 16 August, we made history by hosting a joint celebration of 60 years of independence as a mark of respect for one another's countries.

The forum is non-religious, non-political and has almost become a diplomatic panel with access to both communities at the highest levels. But we also celebrate our common history with cultural events and in doing so add to the growing profile of Asian culture in the UK.

Every year there is an Indian festival in Trafalgar Square and the British people have become used to Asians celebrating festivals such as Diwali, Eid and Vaisakhi. During Vaisakhi we mark the birth of the brotherhood of Sikhs on 13 April with Bhangra music and dancing in Trafalgar Square. In the UK, we are not fighting for a homeland and we are free to celebrate what unites us. The partition of India may have divided us geographically but we must be pragmatic and accept it as a historical fact and deal with it in the best way we can. We have paid the price of colonialism but that is history. Our destinies in the UK are now interlinked and we should not allow the next generation to carry our baggage.

Asians are very much a part of modern Britain, yet there are still barriers that have to be broken down – particularly in politics where I have worked very hard to correct the under-representation of Asians in parliament and their engagement with the wider political process. I first joined the Conservative Party in 1977, when I lived in Sidcup. My MP at the time was the late Sir Edward Heath, who had been the prime minister until 1975. Sir Edward encouraged me to join the local Sidcup and Bexley Business Club, which I did because I thought that I could make connections that would help me get on in business. There were very few Asian members but I accepted this and got on with it; after all, we were still establishing ourselves commercially and socially then.

When I moved to Harrow in 1981, my local MP was another Conservative, the late Sir Rhodes Boyson. He had a Parliamentary Club which I joined and once again I found very few Asian faces, even though there were plenty of Asians living in the area. Instead, the club members were mainly white, public-school educated men who worked as stockbrokers, barristers and the like. It was an elite group – the classic old schoolboy network – and I found them condescending and bigoted. After talking to other Asians in the area, some who were also members of the party, it seemed clear to me that Asians weren't taken seriously by the Tories. Even in areas where Asians were in the majority, we were never selected as parliamentary candidates.

I wondered whether I still wanted to be a member of a party that seemed to be so prejudiced against ethnic minorities. I could have just got my head down and got on with it as I did in other areas of life when faced with prejudice. But that was part of the problem – we Asians were so used to just putting our heads down and giving our time to our work, families and our own communities that we weren't engaging actively enough with the wider community. I realised that this approach to living in Britain wasn't enough to get us noticed at a political level. Politics isn't like business, where you headhunt the best people for the job; it's almost the opposite – in politics people often undermine others to surge ahead. They have vested interests and use family connections and the old schoolboy network to close their 'clubs' to outsiders. We Asians didn't have these advantages, yet we deserved representation. In any democracy, people have a share and political parties should reflect the make-up of modern day Britain. We all have something to contribute, but if we don't have a platform, nobody will get to know us.

If we wanted to break into the clubs and associations and get a proper representation for the three million Asians living in Britain, we needed to act. I felt I had a cause and that the Conservative Party needed me even if it didn't realise it. I made it my personal aim to force them to change.

By now I was in contact with other Asian Conservatives. One of them, Ranbir Suri, a senior party member, felt as passionately as I did that the Conservative Party needed more Asian faces at the highest levels. Along with other prominent Asian Conservatives, we co-founded the British Asian Conservative Link in 1997 to articulate our concerns to the party hierarchy and to raise the profile of Asians in politics. Our aim was to give a platform to the many Asians who were naturally Conservatives but who felt shut out of the political process. We wanted the Conservative Party to see that we were good doctors, accountants and businesspeople and that the Asian community was no longer struggling but was making a valuable contribution to British life. We deserved to have our aspirations and experience recognised and represented in the country's parliament. What's more, we were now successful and influential. We could donate to the party, fundraise, increase awareness and support. We could help the Tory Party modernise and become electable again. In a democracy everyone has a vote, regardless of their race, colour, religion, education or wealth. A vote to a rival party was in effect a loss of two votes to us.

We also wanted to make the Asian community aware that they had a right to participate in the political process and to be represented in the parliament so that they could do more to determine their own futures as decision-makers. Our own people were also at fault for not understanding that a tree without roots could not survive for long. We needed to put down stronger roots in the country we had moved into, be less insular and take a bigger part in deciding how our country should be run.

In 2004, I put myself forward as a parliamentary candidate for Southall in West London, where 60 per cent of the population is Asian. I passed my preliminary test to become an approved candidate and I made sure I got the backing of the Southall community. Then I went for a selection interview with the local Conservative Association in Southall to see if they would have me as their candidate. I made a passionate speech stressing that I had the backing of the community and I truly represented them. But the panel wasn't interested and they rejected me. I felt very aggrieved about this and worried that the party I supported wasn't keeping in step with modern Britain. People were by now saying openly that the Conservative Party was the 'nasty' party.

But we pressed on and the British Asian Conservative Link grew in size and prominence. Gradually we changed minds and attitudes. Sixteen years after its foundation the Conservative Party has five Asian MPs and many more Asian members sitting in the House of Lords, councils, school governing bodies and local associations. In 2007, ten years after forming the BACL, the Conservatives in Ealing and Southall finally selected an Asian candidate for election. For the General Election in 2010, every political party had an Asian candidate in the constituency.

We succeeded in breaking the mould of the Conservative Party, a mould that had remained more or less unchanged for centuries. Our cause was helped with the election of David Cameron as party leader in 2005. He was young, modern and forward-thinking and has made it more possible for ethnic minorities to become parliamentary candidates by changing the system of selection at local level. It's a big victory for all Britons of overseas origin who are making lives as British citizens. It's a massive victory and means the BACL is no longer needed and that the Conservative Party is stronger and Britain richer as a whole. I think that my father would have been proud.

13. REWARDS AND PASSING ON MY WISDOM

I HAVE ACHIEVED a great deal in my 66 years and two of the proudest moments in my life have involved me being given awards by Her Majesty the Queen – my first Queen's Award for Export in 1999 and my MBE in 2005. Every year, Her Majesty gives a reception to the Queen's Award winners in Buckingham Palace to thank them for what they've done for the UK with their businesses. I've been to several now, of course, but I'll never forget the first time. It was more than a sense of arrival. Here I was, a poor immigrant who at times didn't even have a bicycle and who had watched the coronation on television thousands of miles away in India. Now I was walking down the red carpet at Buckingham Palace and being presented to the Queen, our head of state. I could barely believe it was happening.

I arrived at Buckingham Palace with my wife in my battered Toyota Previa and the guard at the gate thought I was her driver. "You can stay with your car there," he told me, pointing to a parking area full of BMWs and Mercedes. "Oh," I replied, "but I'm also going to the reception. I'm a guest." It didn't bother me that I didn't have a high grade executive car like so many of the other award recipients because I knew that I'd earned the honour by not spending money I didn't have on things which I could do without. I wasn't one of those who set up a company and went straight out to get a BMW on lease because I needed to project an image that wasn't real. I could never spend other people's money like that. I knew that if I kept on working and building the business and if I was lucky enough to be given another Queen's Award, then I might be able to arrive at Buckingham Palace in an expensive car paid for with my own money and efforts. So, even though I was in a battered Toyota Previa and they thought I was my wife's driver for the day, I was extremely proud. It was the vehicle that had helped me build my business.

Shaking hands with the Queen was a fantastic honour. She was so gracious and spent two hours on her feet going around every single award winner talking to them and finding out about their business. She's an amazing woman and we're lucky to have her. She does so much for Britain and has helped this small country punch above its weight internationally. This is a great nation. You only have to look at the 2012 Olympics to realise what Britain can achieve when it applies itself. They were the best Olympics by far and we achieved results in a civilised manner without exploiting anyone or bulldozing underprivileged areas or displacing thousands of people to make way for stadiums. Just look at the medals Britain won, too. We are a nation of just 60 million people, yet we came third in the medal table. In terms of population and size, we achieved far more than either the USA or China who were above us.

We are a nation that punches above its weight and this nation has given me the freedom to pursue my ambitions and realise my dreams. I have so much freedom here that I cannot imagine living anywhere else.

I feel very British now and I love the British way of life – it grieves me when people don't appreciate what they've got. Britain contributes great things to the world in sport, business, diplomacy, science, technology and the arts. We also help keep the world safe and secure. Unlike so many other countries, we allow our people to go about their business unhindered. I don't think I could have achieved in India what I have achieved in Britain.

For me, my MBE was the reward for a lifetime of giving back to the community. I run my business the same way I approach my community causes and with the same sense of purpose. With my business, I do good social service by creating wealth and employment and it's driven by the same principles that guide my politics: we can achieve so much more together than separately.

The organisations are of course run by other people, but I am proud to be their figurehead and to publicly represent them and raise awareness for causes that I believe in. Two of the organisations I work with have a particular personal meaning to me. Within the Asian community we have a much higher incidence of strokes and heart disease than the general population. In Harrow alone, for example, heart disease among the majority Asian population is 33 per cent higher than in the Anglo-Irish population and the occurrence of strokes is about twice as high. It's a very serious problem and we all know someone who is affected by it.

Some years ago, when I was with my daughter at Northwick Park Hospital, I met Professor Colin Green, who was the director of the Northwick Park Institute for Medical Research. Colin, a very inspirational man, was passionate about finding reasons behind these conditions. We kept in touch. In 2009, Colin set up a team to conduct research into heart disease and strokes, focusing on a particular kind of protein.

His aim was to establish good diagnostic tools and new treatments for these conditions. Alongside this research, Colin wanted to run a special research project investigating the causes of the high incidence of heart disease and strokes among Asians. He needed at least £200,000 for this project.

I suggested to him that it would be very difficult to find just one donor to give that sort of money and that he might be better off getting it from multiple sources. If we could find 100 people giving £1,000 a year then the costs would be covered. So we formed the Golden Heart Club and I used my connections within the wealthy Asian community to start recruiting members who would pay £1,000 a year for two years. We now have 70 members and we have an annual fundraising dinner along with a sponsored walk. Overall, we're raising more than £100,000 a year for the Heart and Stroke Research Campaign. Colin retired last year and the research project is now being overseen by Professor Shervanthi Homer-Vanniasinkam; it is in very good hands.

The other thing I'm involved in, which is very satisfying, is my work with young people under the umbrella of the Prince's Trust. I give lectures at university business schools and now I am a fellow for the trust. The Prince's Trust mentors and supports young people from underprivileged backgrounds and encourages them to stand up on their own feet. It also helps them to start their own business by providing loans and practical support under the banner of the Enterprise Fellowship. Along with more than 40 other successful entrepreneurs, I help to fund the trust's enterprise programme. I raise awareness of their work and share my knowledge and experience with young people who are starting out on their business journey as I did more than 25 years ago. It's so important to act as a role model and to inspire young people who have not had the best start in life. If I can turn a liability into an asset, that to me is a great achievement.

So, three or four times a year I give talks to young entrepreneurs and business students in which I tell them my story and explain that you don't need a rich father or an elite education to succeed in life. What you do need, however, is vision, self-respect, ethics, total commitment and empathy for others. I answer questions and share the wisdom I have accrued through more than 40 years of working in and running my own businesses. I have included the text of one of my speeches at the end of this chapter because it sums up what I have learned during my years of working and running businesses in Britain and what I would like to pass on to others who are just starting out on their journey as I was in 1971. Perhaps it's what I would like someone to have told me back then when I was sleeping on my brother's living room floor and the realisation was dawning on me that perhaps life wasn't going to be as easy as I had imagined.

I find this work very satisfying, not least because it means that I am working alongside the Prince of Wales, who himself is an excellent role model for business people like me. The Prince has time for people who come from disadvantaged backgrounds. He gives them hope and gets people like me on board to help them overcome their struggles. Like me, he believes that we have a responsibility to turn what some people might consider liabilities into assets.

In this, as in everything I do in life and work, I am inspired by Mahatma Gandhi and more so by the Sikh Gurus and my own father. Gandhi's life work and words have inspired me throughout life. Here was a man who was a barrister from a good family but who gave it all up for a cause. In doing so, he not only changed the destiny of more than a billion Indians but I believe the world. Without Gandhi, there would be no Nelson Mandela, no Martin Luther King and no Barack Obama. His influence has been profound and widespread. Who else has had a stamp issued bearing his likeness in 100 countries without being a king?

In my political and social cohesion projects and my work with young entrepreneurs I am guided by the words attributed to Gandhi: *"Be the change you wish to see in the world".* I want to make an impact beyond the world of business and in my own humble way I would like to bring change and see a better Britain for the generations after us. Many people in my position live, breathe, sleep and think business – and that's all they do. They are ignorant of the wider community around them – it's just business, business and more business for them. They do very well and make lots of money and feel good about their business success. But that's not the case for me. I don't want to be just a successful businessman; however, being a successful businessman gives me the platform to pursue other projects. Why should I not use my influence to benefit others and help bring together divided communities at home? Even in my support for Combat Stress, the charity that supports British soldiers returning from overseas with post-traumatic stress disorder, I am giving something back to the community that has enabled me to become the man I am.

Business was a challenge which I have conquered to some degree and I feel that I can carry on growing and growing. But my charitable work, my community work – these are never-ending challenges and they bring me into contact with a much wider range of people than business alone can do. They broaden my experience and my knowledge of the world and enable me to leave my mark. I have been blessed with the qualities that make me a good businessman and I feel a great obligation to use these qualities in the service of others. There are so many other aspects of society that I cannot just ignore and I believe that if you are good in one field, you can be good in another too. You may not be perfect but you will be good. And if you take the qualities that made you a success in the first place and apply them elsewhere, you are bound to achieve results.

A speech given by Rami Ranger to MBA students of Hertford University on 29 October 2009

Ladies and Gentlemen,

I am grateful to Professor Tim Wilson for giving me this opportunity to share my story with you and to Muditha Cooray and Alison Cole for making all the arrangements.

It is indeed encouraging to see that so many of you are preparing for the challenges of life.

Before I begin, I would like to ask you a simple question: How is it that two medical students who attend the same university, read the same books and are taught by the same professors for the same length of time, end up practising in two very different places – one in Harley Street and the other in some backstreet carrying out dodgy operations?

The answer is simple: the one practising in Harley Street takes time to understand his patients and in establishing the cause of an ailment and the method of treatment. Unfortunately, the doctor who practises in the backstreets cannot be bothered with this and is just after quick rewards.

Similarly, we must work hard to be the best amongst the rest by going the extra mile.

Mediocrity will not bring us the desired result. We may be able to get by, but we will not make a mark, nor will we be noticed by others unless we are perfectionists.

They say, "*Excellence endures; it remains long after everything else is forgotten.*"

I am here to share my story with you, so that you can understand that to be successful and to realise one's ambitions, one does not need to have wealthy parents or the old schoolboy network.

My father was assassinated two months before my birth by religious fanatics as he was against the division of India on the basis of religion. If to lose a breadwinner was not enough in a poor country, we also lost our ancestral home and country and became refugees due to the division of India in 1947.

You can well imagine the hardships we must have faced growing up in a refugee camp. We were eight siblings with a remarkable mother who worked as a teacher in a junior school and brought us up through immense difficulties.

I feel that there are certain things essential to succeed in life. It is a pre-requisite to have self-respect, ethics, empathy for others and above all, total commitment to work. I not only demand that of myself, but also of those who work with me.

I am a great believer in customer service. It is essential that we work for the success of our customers as their success in turn becomes our success.

Empathy for others is essential. No company can grow if their customers are suffering because of our "I'm all right Jack" approach. If we treat our customers right, then we will build our reputation which is essential for our business to grow and flourish.

Those who evade taxes or cut corners to save money can never grow to be a world-class company.

Many of you will start your career by working for others and many of you may move into your own business. If you start in the family business, my suggestion to you is to first learn the ropes from the bottom up. That way you will learn from your personal experience what is essential to build a strong foundation, before taking on extra responsibilities at a later stage.

For those who start their careers working for others, you should always work as if it is your own business, otherwise you will only work when you are being watched and as a result will not develop your true potential. Those who watch the clock instead of their work continue to do so whilst others who watch their work surge ahead.

We must take pride in what ever job we do. If we are not fit for a small job, then we cannot be fit for a bigger one.

We must have the ability to get on with our seniors and juniors alike and must never become an opposition leader to our superiors. Instead, we should try and take some pressure off them and act as a pressure valve easing their workload. The result is that our superiors will always like to work with us rather than those who give them lip and induce unnecessary pressure.

Our attitude towards our juniors should be such that we should take time to explain the rationale behind our instructions, so that they too can appreciate where we are coming from, rather than expecting them to be mere typewriters. We must make them feel important and encourage them to do more and help them to grow and develop so that they too can become assets.

We must always add value to whatever we do. For example, anyone can serve at McDonald's, but the person who serves with charm and politeness will be noticed and bring respect not only to the establishment, but also to himself.

We must always try to mix with people who are more successful than us. By standing in short grass, we appear to look tall but, in fact, we are not.

It is paramount to join bodies and organisations that represent the field we are going to be in, as this will keep us abreast of what is going on. This also offers us the opportunity to network with the right people.

Hidden talent is no talent and we must market ourselves as much as possible, so that people know what we can offer and what benefits we can provide.

They say common sense is not so common, so we must apply as much common sense as possible in order to complement our academic qualifications when making decisions. Having educational qualifications is one thing, but to have vision and ambition is another.

My suggestion to you is that you must watch programmes such as *Newsnight* to learn from the experiences of successful people and, above all, their ability to answer barrages of questions designed to trip them up.

The difference between success and failure is simple: a successful man works hard to benefit others, so that he is liked and respected; whereas a failure regards it as his divine right to be loved and respected by everyone, regardless of his own attitude and behaviour. We must always remain an asset and never become a liability to anyone, whether they are our employers or suppliers.

I can summarise my approach to business with the following analogy: our approach to business must never be like a hunter who likes to go in for a quick kill; instead, our approach should be like that of a farmer who works hard for a bumper harvest over time.

Before I conclude, I would like to pay tribute to my adopted country, Great Britain. It is because of British tolerance and sense of fair play that an ordinary person like me could succeed and fulfil his ambitions.

Any country which discriminates against a section of her population purely on the basis of colour, religion or race, cannot progress. We must never turn assets into liabilities for ourselves simply by being unfair.

Finally, there is a widely held belief amongst us Indians that we are smarter than the English.

A visiting Indian leader was once invited to dinner with Sir Winston Churchill. When Churchill came back after his speech, the Indian leader plucked up courage and said to the then British prime minister:

"Sir, I am afraid you speak grammatically incorrect English."

Churchill was flabbergasted, to say the least.

He looked at this small man in disbelief and said, "My dear sir, when an Englishman speaks, the grammar just follows him."

Thank you.

PART IV. EVERYTHING

14. EVERYTHING

A S SUN MARK has grown, my role in the business has changed. I am less involved in the day-to-day management now and more occupied by the strategic thinking and decision-making that sets the direction of the business. I spend much of my working time thinking about our next moves, such as launching new products, entering new markets and building strategic alliances. I also act as the figurehead for the business, representing Sun Mark at dinners, award ceremonies and in the media.

What I do now is a far cry from the days when I was on my feet for 12 hours or more a day running a small shop or when I was doing absolutely everything myself as the founder of a new business in the self-storage shed in Hayes. Even as my businesses have grown, I have remained very hands-on and am always concerned about attention to detail. This is in my nature. Even though my role has become more strategic – a natural development for the leader of a growing business – I have not always found it easy to delegate some of the tasks and responsibilities that I have always considered my own. Of course, entrepreneurs like me always think we can do things better than anyone else. To trust other people to do something well even if they don't do it in the same way isn't easy. But it is necessary in order to progress a business.

Recently, the evolution of my role has been accelerated by circumstances. As I write, I am emerging from an ordeal. This time it was triggered by my decision to challenge a giant in the drinks world, Red Bull, over its trademarking practices. Our dispute has taken more than ten years to resolve and has been very stressful, time-consuming and costly for me. I was found guilty by the court of infringing Red Bull's trademark. It was a humiliating experience, with huge financial implications to me and to my business. The experience has left me exhausted. In hindsight, I see that I took a stand on a matter of principle that perhaps I shouldn't have taken and my insistence on my principles could have ruined Sun Mark had we not finally reached an amicable out-of-court agreement with Red Bull.

Unlike when I was a single guy making my way in the world, I have a great deal to lose now; so many people have come to depend on my judgement. I have to be their leader, their captain and I can't take chances with so much resting on my decisions. My error of judgement could have put the livelihoods of my employees and even my customers at risk. If I were to give myself some advice now it would be, 'If you take a stand on principle, just make sure that the stand does not have the potential to ruin your business and the future of those who depend on you.'

It has been a humbling experience to find that even at the age of 66 I have more to learn. But it's also been a necessary lesson and a warning to me that I cannot carry on pushing myself as I did when I was a young and healthy 40-year-old. There comes a time when, like a striker in football, it is harder to score with the same regularity that you have grown used to. I have always worked at a high pace because I have wanted to prove myself. But over the last year I have been asking myself the question: 'What more do I have to prove?' I have built a £180-million-a-year business from scratch, won six Queen's Awards, been awarded an MBE and many other accolades. I have everything. What more do I have to prove?

The months since the dispute with Red Bull ended have been a time for recovery and reflection. Just as when I was trying to balance too many responsibilities while working at Dixons almost 30 years ago, I have had to accept that my mind and my body had slipped out of synch with each other. My mind wanted to keep pushing, keep fighting – as is my character. However, with the stress of litigation, along with the pressure of running the business and keeping up with my community activities, I found that my body just couldn't cope. Once again, I felt a deep fatigue and my confidence drained away. I was fortunate that my previous experience of coping with stress helped me to understand what was happening and why.

As before, I took comfort from my Sikh faith, which teaches us that we must all learn to live in the conditions that manifest themselves; if we lose a leg, we must learn how to live without it and not constantly dwell on the loss of a limb. I accepted that I was not invincible and had neglected my body over many years and now needed to pay more attention to my physical wellbeing. I never used to worry about having breakfast in the morning, for example. It was all rush, rush, rush. But now I make a point of having vitamins and fruit first thing. I eat more salads and vegetables. I exercise more. However busy our lives are and however great the pressure we feel, we must always take the time to take care of ourselves. We're not unbreakable even if we think we are.

There's no quick fix to exhaustion. It takes time to get used to the new phenomena you experience and with time it becomes a norm. One must not panic, as panic leads to more panic. One must accept that what cannot be cured must be endured, like we accept bereavement in the family or the loss of a limb. We all catch colds and we all get better too. We simply have to give it time and do the right things, such as removing the causes of stress from our lives if we can. I have started working shorter hours and have handed over the day-to-day running of the business to my son-in-law, Harmeet, who has been my right-hand man for years and is doing an excellent job as managing director. His accomplishment has shown me that I can afford to take a back-seat now and deal more with planning rather than getting involved with every detail. I've realised that perhaps it is time to slow down a little and enjoy the other things that life has to offer.

This new approach to business is working: I am recovering my energy and my enthusiasm for life and I feel different now. I have had time to think about everything I've learned and everything that life has given me. I have travelled such a long way from that small, cramped house in Patiala and my journey has literally been from nothing to everything.

Nowadays I live in a comfortable house in a smart neighbourhood in west London and I own both a Mercedes and a Rolls-Royce rather than the Toyota Previa that took me to Buckingham Palace for my first Queen's Award in 1999. My marriage is strong and I have three wonderful daughters who make me proud. I no longer need material things in life.

In fact, you could say that the world is my oyster. My principles have not really changed from the days when I was running small shops to now, where the scale of business has expanded massively. In those days, my market was limited by geographical areas and my customers spent less. But even if a child came in with just five pence to spend, I would give him the same amount of attention as anyone else. His five pence was very important to him and to me.

Nowadays, I go to trade shows in Frankfurt and San Francisco and my customers are all over the globe. But my commitment to service remains the same, whether my customer is spending £500 or £50,000, and I am as happy as I was when I had nothing or just £100 in my till. What matters are the values that you bring to your work and your life. These are what give you self-respect, not the amount of money you have in the bank or the size of the car you drive.

These are the values I instil in my daughters. I am content that there is no need for them to undergo the same journey I have, but it's important to me that they take nothing for granted and live their own lives with good principles and a sense of self-respect. My eldest daughter, Reena, is a mother now and is married to Harmeet. Like me, she supports social causes and has started her own organisation, Women Empowered, to inspire women to take up business, the arts and public life. She is also an approved parliamentary candidate for the Conservative Party and is looking for a seat. Amita, my middle daughter, studied medicine and graduate with honours from Imperial College. Now she is a haematologist and is married to an orthopaedic surgeon, Sanjeeve. My youngest daughter, Sabina, is just 20 and studying business economics at a leading university. She works so hard that sometimes I find myself asking her, "Sabina, why are you working so hard when you are going to inherit the fruits of a successful business?" But like her sisters, she has so much self-respect that she wants to prove to me and to everyone else that she has the intelligence and application to be successful in her own right. I am very proud of my daughters.

They have ambition like me. I am still driven even though I am making the decision to slow down. Although I know I have everything, I still feel I am the same small humble guy that ran convenience stores and started a small freight-forwarding company in modest surroundings on an industrial estate in west London. Sometimes I forget what I have achieved and it's only when I see the response of the people I meet that I remember. But ambition is like this – no matter what you've built, you see the potential to build something bigger. I started with the ambition of buying one suit, then I wanted to buy another and then another. My family says I have inherited my father's qualities and I am very privileged if I have. He was a larger-than-life character and people respected him because he was such an active person in so many fields. If I am half the man my father was, I should be satisfied.

We only live once in this world and we haven't the luxury of wasting time. Although my life has not gone as I imagined it would when I was a young man heading for England, where I believed the streets were paved with gold, it has worked out very well.

Although I am content with what I have achieved, when I think about the business I am still excited. I still want more. I still see potential for growth and opportunities to diversify into new areas. I see no reason why Sun Mark cannot continue to experience double-digit growth and reach a turnover of half a billion pounds within five years. We are stretching our brands all the time and still venturing into new markets where economies are growing, such as Mongolia. There are new customers to be won, new accounts to be created and new territories to open up. They say that when the river starts to flow it takes in all the surrounding areas, and the model I have created for my business means that with the right leader at the helm, it will keep growing and growing. The thought of this ignites my ambition again and makes me want to build more and more. But perhaps the responsibility of carrying Sun Mark into the future is realistically a task for someone else.

Besides, I have found myself giving more and more time to my community causes and this along with my family is where I think my own future lies. I have a great sense of social responsibility and consider it my duty to pass on my wisdom to business students and in particular to disadvantaged young people who are trying to start their own enterprises. I identify with them strongly. I was there too, once, and it seems such a short time ago. If I can do anything that will give young people a solid platform for pursuing their own business ambitions, then I will. It's so important that as adults with knowledge and experience we don't keep it to ourselves but pass it on to those who need it most.

I'm not an extremely religious man but I love my religion for the practical things it has given the world. The inspiration of the Sikh Gurus who gave up their lives in support of their principles such as religious freedom, social equality and sharing one's fortune with those who are less fortunate inspires me. I have always believed that deeds speak louder than words and our actions should be to the benefit of all, wherever possible.

Nothing is ideal in this world but we have to make the most of what we have when we have it. In doing so, we should strive for whatever right we can do. If we do nothing, we achieve nothing. As I often say, efforts are in the hands of man, rewards are in the hand of God. So we must continue to make the effort and then I believe everything will work out for the best. Or, as Mahatma Gandhi put it, in words that bear repeating again and again: *"Be the change you want to see in the world"*.

DR RAMI RANGER MBE, FRSA: LIST OF ACHIEVEMENTS

Awards

Queen's Award for Export 1999

Queen's Award for Enterprise 2009, 2010, 2011, 2012, 2013

MBE for services to British Business and the Asian Community 2005

Honorary Doctorate for Contribution to Business from Preston University in Wyoming USA

Director of the Year for Large Business in London and South East Region 2012, Institute of Directors

Community Service Award 2012, GOPIO (Global Organisation of People of Indian Origin)

Business Person of the Year 2011, Asian Achievers Awards

Asian Business of the Year Award 2011, Eastern Eye website

Entrepreneur of the Year Award 2010, *Asian Voice* newspaper

Business & Commerce Award 2009, Lloyds TSB

Community Service Award, Indian Association UK

Special award for increasing bilateral trade and business investment between the UK and India, Indo British Partnership

Award for Industry, India International Foundation

The NRI (Non Resident Indian) honour for contribution to business

Community Award 2008, GG2 Leadership Awards

Community Service Award 2008, Asian Voice newspaper

Pride of India Award 2008, Punjabi Society of British Isles

Finalist in the Ernst Young Entrepreneur of the Year Award 2008

Joint Winner of the Real Business Growing Business Awards Export Champion of the Year 2013

Contributions to community

Fellow of the Prince's Trust

Co-founder of British Asian Conservative Link

Founder member of Hindu Forum Britain

Co-founder and chairman of the Pakistan, India & UK Friendship Forum

Chairman of the British Sikh Association

President of the Punjabi Society of the British Isles

Chairman of the British Sikh Association

Co-founder and chairman of the Golden Heart Club

Member of the Memorial Gates Commemoration Committee

Patron of HAVEN, a British charity providing medical and educational facilities to poor and needy people in India

Patron of the India International Foundation, which celebrates success of Indians in Britain

Patron of the Shaheed Nanak Singh Foundation, which encourages British Indians to become more public and politically spirited

Patron of the Ethnic Minority Business Group

Supporter of Combat Stress, providing support to British armed forces veterans with psychological wounds

AFTERWORD
BY RICHARD HARRINGTON

I DO HOPE this book is read by many people. They should not read it for thrills or entertainment. They should not read it for 'get rich quick' tips or business ideas to copy. The book should, in my view, be read for one reason – to get inspiration for your own life.

This is important, because many of us were born with advantages in life that Rami Ranger did not have. We may have been born with a stable family life, in a peaceful, prosperous country. We may have been born to a family with money or with all the advantages of a high quality, uninterrupted education.

However, most of us need many things, luck, judgement; friends are important, I agree. However, in my life, in 30 years of business and a few in politics, the most important thing for any of us is the influence of one person. That person is the one who inspires us to achieve what we can in life. Some of us meet that person, indeed it may be a member of family or close friend. However, for many of us, that person is a person that we never personally know, that we read about in newspapers or see on TV.

I believe that is the main reason people should read this book. Rami Ranger is a hugely inspiring man. Read his story and become obsessed with being like him. It is a hard task, but this book shows that with the right motivation, effort and determination, a man born without the advantages of many can succeed hugely and inspire others.

Please read it and benefit from it. It could transform your life.

Rt Hon Richard Harrington MP

Vice Chairman of the Conservative Party